RISING CURRENTS
Projects for New York's Waterfront

BARRY BERGDOLL

RISING CURRENTS

PROJECTS FOR NEW YORK'S WATERFRONT

The Museum of Modern Art, New York

Published in conjunction with the exhibition *Rising Currents: Projects for New York's Waterfront*, March 24–October 11, 2010, at The Museum of Modern Art, New York, organized by Barry Bergdoll, The Philip Johnson Chief Curator of Architecture and Design. The exhibition and publication were made possible by the Rockefeller Foundation. *Rising Currents* was the first of five exhibitions in the series Issues in Contemporary Architecture, supported by Andre Singer.

Produced by the Department of Publications, The Museum of Modern Art, New York

Edited by Rebecca Roberts with Libby Hruska and Claire Barliant
Designed by Hsien-Yin Ingrid Chou
Cover design by Hsien-Yin Ingrid Chou and Vance Wellenstein
Production by Tiffany Hu

Printed and bound by Main Choice International Development Ltd.

This book is typeset in DIN. The paper is 140 gsm Japanese Ex-Grade woodfree and 150 gsm Mori Silk.

Library of Congress Control Number: 2011931595
ISBN: 978-0-87070-807-7

Published by The Museum of Modern Art
11 West 53 Street, New York, NY 10019-5497
www.moma.org

Distributed in the United States and Canada by D.A.P./Distributed Art Publishers, Inc.
155 Sixth Avenue, 2nd Floor
New York, NY 10013
www.artbook.com

Distributed outside the United States and Canada by Thames & Hudson, Ltd.
181 High Holborn, London WC1V 7QX
www.thamesandhudson.com

Printed in China

The *Rising Currents* blog is part of the project website, at MoMA.org/risingcurrents.

Water Proving Ground
Liberty State Park [80]

Working Waterline
Kill Van Kull and
Bayonne, New Jersey [70]

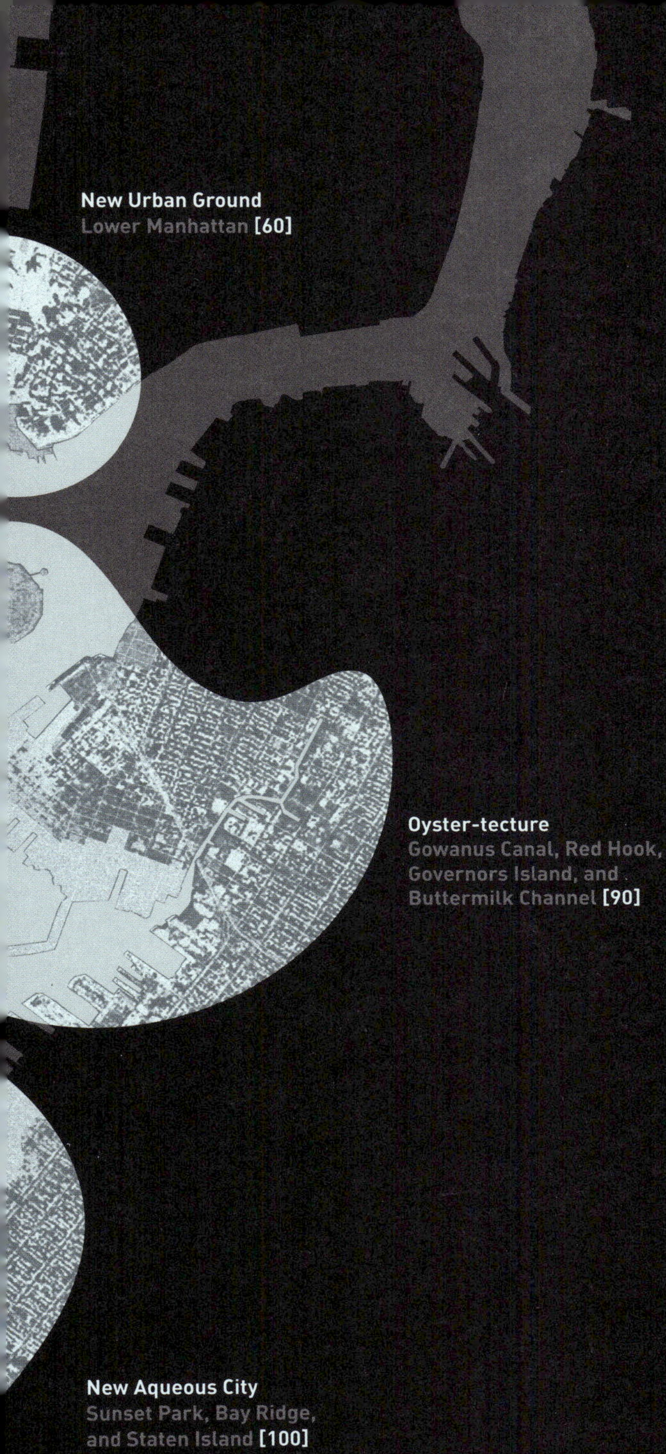

New Urban Ground
Lower Manhattan [60]

Oyster-tecture
Gowanus Canal, Red Hook,
Governors Island, and
Buttermilk Channel [90]

New Aqueous City
Sunset Park, Bay Ridge,
and Staten Island [100]

TABLE OF CONTENTS

LIBERTY STATE PARK
TEAM LEADERS:
Paul Lewis, Marc Tsurumaki, and David J. Lewis,
LTL Architects

TEAM MEMBERS:
Aaron Forrest
Megan Griscom, OPEN Landscape Architecture
Perla Dis Kristinsdóttir, LTL Architects
Yasmin Vobis

KILL VAN KULL AND BAYONNE
TEAM LEADER:
Matthew Baird, Matthew Baird Architects

TEAM MEMBERS:
Kira Appelhans
Kristen Becker
Nim Lee
Ajay Manthripragada
Mario Milana del Bosch

FOREWORD

Even in light of The Museum of Modern Art's history as an advocate of cutting-edge research and social advocacy in architecture, *Rising Currents: Projects for New York's Waterfront* has been a bold experiment. In the years since its founding, in 1929, the Museum has urged designers and administrators to channel the profession's explorations toward the important challenges of the moment. In the 1930s the newly created Department of Architecture played a key role in the housing debates and legislation of the time with a series of exhibitions including *Housing Exhibition of the City of New York* (1934); it furthered this role in 1967 with *The New City: Architecture and Urban Renewal*, a landmark critique of inner-city transformation through large-scale demolition. In *Rising Currents*, a rejuvenation of this tradition, the Museum set one of the most urgent problems in design today—ameliorating the effects of global climate change—before five interdisciplinary teams of architects, landscape architects, engineers, ecologists, and artists, committing to exhibit the results even before design work had begun.

Rising Currents calls for the reinvention of urban infrastructure in the face of the effects of rising sea level on the world's great cities, many of which are situated in low-lying coastal areas. It is the first exhibition in MoMA's new Issues in Contemporary Architecture series, in which the Museum will take a leadership role in responding to contemporary developments and demands. In collaboration with MoMA PS1, the project also inaugurated the workshop-exhibition, making studio spaces that have long served artists available to architects and designers, thus putting creative and cutting-edge design work in direct contact with policy makers and the public.

This publication presents the five teams' proposals for New York City and is a record of the lively discourse around urban infrastructure design that took place during the workshop, throughout the exhibition at MoMA, and on the interactive pages of the project's website.

Rising Currents open houses and events attracted visitors at every level, from interested citizens to officials of the city, state, and federal governments, and the project's influence is already in evidence—it is acknowledged, for example, in 2011 planning documents of the New York City Department of City Planning. This volume is intended to extend the impact of *Rising Currents* so that it may serve architecture students, public officials, designers, and others who work in areas that demand interdisciplinary thinking.

Barry Bergdoll, The Philip Johnson Chief Curator of Architecture and Design, conceived *Rising Currents* and ably organized it from inception to realization, aided by Emma Presler, Department Manager, Department of Architecture and Design. I am grateful to him for bringing this precedent-setting project to fruition and to Guy Nordenson, Catherine Seavitt, and Adam Yarinksy, authors of the 2007–09 study *On The Water: Palisade Bay,* which provided both the data and the manifesto on which the entire experiment was based. On behalf of the staff and trustees of the Museum, I would like to thank Andre Singer and the Rockefeller Foundation for their indispensible support of the exhibition and this publication.

Glenn D. Lowry
DIRECTOR, THE MUSEUM OF MODERN ART

20FT

Projected sea-level rise with a category 3 storm surge. A storm surge is a short-term high-water level caused by a weather event. A category 3 storm surge is greater than a category 1 storm surge.

10FT

Projected sea-level rise with a 500-year flood. If sea levels returned to their 1971–2000 average, a flood of this magnitude would occur once in every 500 years. As sea levels rise, the likelihood of such a flood rises as well. For example, at average sea levels predicted for the 2080s, a "500-year" flood will occur once every 120–250 years.

8FT

Projected sea-level rise with a 100-year flood. If sea levels returned to their 1971–2000 average, a flood of this magnitude would occur once in every 100 years. As sea levels rise, the likelihood of such a flood rises as well. For example, at average sea levels predicted for the 2080s, a "100-year" flood will occur once every 15–35 years.

6FT

Projected sea-level rise by 2100.

5FT 8IN

Projected sea-level rise with a c
A storm surge is a short-term h
by a weather event. A category
than a category 1 storm surge.

4FT

Projected sea-level rise by 2080 with Rapid Ice M
Scenario. Rapid Ice Melt Scenario is a model th
incorporates long-term historical ice-melt r
based on both the recent acceleration of ic
the Greenland and West Antarctic ice she
on paleoclimate studies.

2FT

Projected sea-le

PREFACE

For millions of people around the world, the consequences of climate change will become increasingly evident and increasingly devastating. Higher temperatures will create more droughts and lead to the spread of heat-related diseases. Harsher storms will lead to flooding and the loss of crops and safe drinking water. All of this, taken together, will mean the destruction of homes, jobs, food, and—tragically—lives.

This prediction, though dire, is an opportunity. *Rising Currents: Projects for New York's Waterfront* confronts the threat of climate change head-on, turning the risks into incentives to create a more inviting, livable, and resilient world. In 2009–10, five multidisciplinary teams of architects, landscape architects, engineers, ecologists, and artists were challenged to reenvision areas of coastline around New York City in light of rising sea level and more frequent extreme weather events—the results of climate change. Their proposals, presented in this volume, paint a picture of a dynamic, flexible, and green city, a city in which new juxtapositions of water and land form recreation spaces, native plant species flourish in their original habitats, and toxic sites have been repurposed into clean-energy hubs. Lower Manhattan is a Venetian landscape, in which amphibious "green" streets are lined with porous pavement. Giant interlocking forms made of recycled glass slow coastal storm surges, an aquatic amphitheater rises out of the water, and the Bay Ridge Flats are once again inhabited by oyster beds, which decelerate storm currents and cleanse the river. These innovative design solutions were conceived in an architects-in-residence program and design workshop led by Barry Bergdoll, The Philip Johnson Chief Curator of Architecture and Design at The Museum of Modern Art, New York, hosted by MoMA PS1, in Long Island City, Queens, and financially supported by the Rockefeller Foundation. The teams were visited by city officials, climate scientists, and, during two open houses, members of the public; this feedback was crucial as the designers developed their proposals. The resulting

exhibition at The Museum of Modern Art was organized by the teams in conjunction with Bergdoll.

The Rockefeller Foundation is proud to support this pioneering project as part of our broader initiative to promote climate-change response nationally and internationally. It is our ongoing mission to help the economically vulnerable tap into globalization's benefits and strengthen their resilience to risk, and we are committed to the support of New York City's diverse cultural institutions, which play a fundamental role in promoting innovations that have societal benefits both immediate and long-term. The iterative multidisciplinary design process embodied in this catalogue is the hallmark of effective approaches to complex systems problems. It is a valuable model for citizens, governments, businesses, and others working together to tackle the persistent problems society faces.

And climate change is indeed a complex problem of global proportions. It requires us to fundamentally reconsider where and how we live as societies; demands that we reinvent infrastructure design to meet the more variable conditions cities will face in the future; and necessitates flexibility, resourcefulness, and robust and redundant systems that continue working even when stressed and bounce back rapidly when damaged. The exhibition and this catalogue inspire us to face the climate challenge and transform it into an opportunity for safer and greener cities that are more equitable, livable, and competitive. This is a challenge—and an opportunity—we cannot afford to ignore. We congratulate MoMA and the enterprising design teams featured in *Rising Currents* for opening up a pathway to resilience and inspiring others to follow.

Dr. Judith Rodin
PRESIDENT, THE ROCKEFELLER FOUNDATION

2FT

PROJECTED SEA-LEVEL RISE
BY 2080. THE BAYONNE PIERS
WOULD BE INUNDATED.

ESSAYS

SEPTEMBER 21, 2010

At the US Environmental Protection Agency (EPA),
our mission is to protect human health and the
environment, and taking action on climate change is
a top priority. But the task of mitigating and adapting
to climate change is far bigger than any one agency.
As *Rising Currents* illustrates, this undertaking will
cross jurisdictional boundaries throughout the New
York Harbor and involve contributions from across our
society in ways that transcend conventional thinking.
We welcome creative solutions to this far-reaching
problem and look forward to working together with all
those who strive to create a better future.

—Daniel Teitelbaum, Program Analyst, US EPA Region 2,
New York, on the *Rising Currents* blog

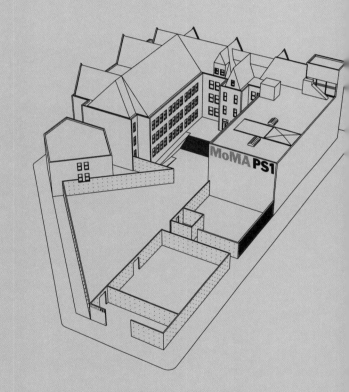

RISING CURRENTS: INCUBATOR FOR DESIGN AND DEBATE **Barry Bergdoll**

MoMA PS1 is The Museum of
Modern Art's contemporary art
affiliate in Long Island City, Queens.

Aspects of the project sites. Top to bottom: Lower Manhattan, Liberty State Park, and the Bayonne, New Jersey, waterfront.

Rising sea level and more frequent and violent storms, the combined effects of global warming, are predicted to create anything from a normative 2-foot rise in the harbor and estuaries of New York City by 2080 to surges of up to 30 feet in a Category 1 storm. *Rising Currents: Projects for New York's Waterfront*—a workshop, an exhibition, and now a book—reimagines the city in light of the future effects of climate change, exploring development now to meet future conditions.

In autumn and winter 2009–10, MoMA PS1, in Long Island City, Queens, hosted five design teams, each an interdisciplinary mix of expertise in architecture, landscape architecture, engineering, ecology, and visual art.[1] Each team was assigned a location in and around New York City and tasked with developing so-called "soft infrastructure" there, proposals that would ameliorate the effects of climate change by mimicking nature and accepting a blurring of the edge between land and water. Over the course of two and a half months, expert advisors and the general public were invited to MoMA PS1 to view and comment on the designs in progress. The teams contributed to a *Rising Currents* website and blog throughout the period, and the project culminated with an exhibition of their work in The Robert B. Menschel Architecture and Design Gallery at The Museum of Modern Art, in March 2010. Even before the projects were completed and installed, the workshop had catalyzed a public and professional following and considerable discussion in the media.

THE MUSEUM

One of my goals upon joining MoMA in 2007 was to find innovative ways to engage with contemporary practice in architecture, landscape architecture, city planning, and design-related engineering, complements to what I call the "reactive" curatorial mode. In the reactive mode, the curator culls from recent or ongoing production what he or she admires and thinks deserves contextualization and wider publicity. It is the traditional role of the curator, developed along with the role of the museum as a showcase for architecture retrospectives.

Now, with the availability at the Museum of MoMA PS1 as a kind of research tank and of the Internet as a way of communicating with the public on an ongoing basis, another approach is possible. There are many issues MoMA could engage more actively and productively, whether identifying and supporting trends in current design or posing questions that have not yet been adequately addressed, be they social, technical, or environmental. In this way, the Museum would not simply research and reflect the production of architecture but would be part of its larger societal role and an actor in the culture of design. This curatorial mode is not completely foreign to MoMA. Since its founding in 1932, the Museum's Department of Architecture (since 1949 the Department of Architecture and Design) has been associated with strong positions and polemical campaigns for change. *Modern Architecture: International Exhibition* (1932) did not simply expose American audiences to the most recent progressive architectural design in Europe; it is too often forgotten that this influential exhibition included a critique of current housing conditions in New York—a critique that in subsequent years the great urban theorist Lewis Mumford and the pioneering housing scholar and advocate Catherine Bauer helped to perfect in exhibitions (notably *Housing Exhibition of the City of New York*, at MoMA in 1934) that led to changes in public policy at both municipal and

Views of *Modern Architecture: International Exhibition*, 1932 (top), and *The New City: Architecture and Urban Renewal*, 1967 (bottom), at The Museum of Modern Art, New York.

Outdoor and indoor sections of *Home Delivery: Fabricating the Modern Dwelling*, 2008, at The Museum of Modern Art, New York.

federal levels.[2] In the late 1960s, the department again engaged the pressing needs of the city, inviting four university-based teams of architects to create counterproposals for four areas of Manhattan and the nearby Bronx slated for massive redevelopment. The resulting exhibition, *The New City: Architecture and Urban Renewal* (1967), sparked a debate in the press and, to a limited extent, among the public.[3] In that episodic tradition, *Home Delivery: Fabricating the Modern Dwelling* (2008) brought reactive and activist curatorial modes together, the latter represented by a series of full-scale, newly commissioned proposals for prefabricated housing, installed on the Museum's vacant lot on West Fifty-third Street in Manhattan, as well as samples of digitally fabricated walls in the introductory gallery of the historical exhibition indoors.[4] The aim was not simply to showcase existing work but also to focus the current excitement about digital fabrication on an issue that has long both fascinated and frustrated modern architects—the serial fabrication of dwellings—engaging both hard technology and computer-guided software to create a new paradigm for the delivery of architecture. In both *Home Delivery* and *Rising Currents* the curatorial teams brought together players who do not frequently collaborate, hoping to stimulate a new interchange—between researchers in prefabrication and digital fabrication, in the former, and between architects, landscape architects, engineers, ecologists, and artists in *Rising Currents*.[5]

THE PROBLEM

Sea level rise is underway around the globe, as oceans warm and glaciers melt. Its seriousness is rendered dramatically clear by the quest—much covered in the press in the last few years—of the Maldives to find a new home for its population of almost 400,000, since the atolls that support the Indian Ocean nation reach their peak at around 8 feet (2.5 m). Rising water levels will change not only the contours of islands but also population patterns around the world, as millions of people in heavily populated areas are directly affected. Ten of the world's fifteen largest cities are in low-lying coastal areas vulnerable to rising sea level or coastal surges, including Shanghai, Mumbai, and Cairo. In the Mekong Delta, home to some 17 million people, more than one-third of the land area will be underwater if government reports are correct. They predict a sea level rise in the Gulf of Thailand of as much as 3 feet (almost 1 m) within the next few decades. The most conservative estimates predict that at least one-fifth of the delta will be inundated.[6] Rapid climate change is overwhelming the arrangements that, in the past, allowed countries to cope with floods and storm surges. Today the Netherlands spends around $100 per person per year on flood defenses; in Bangladesh, a country prone to dangerous flooding, that sum is one-quarter of the average annual income for an individual.[7] The opening up of year-round ice-free channels in the Arctic, as glaciers melt, is changing patterns of trade, creating potential new geopolitical rivalries, and displacing populations—and not only of endangered polar bears.

Recent efforts to heighten public awareness of these facts and to engage the design community have extended from science museums and academic conferences to the studios of architecture schools. The Norwegian National Museum of Science, Technology, and Medicine in Oslo recently presented *Klima X* (Climate X, 2007–09), an exhibition in which visitors donned rubber boots to negotiate a flooded room containing melting blocks of ice symbolizing the Arctic ice cap.[8] In 2009 the National Gallery of Modern Art, Mumbai, presented the exhibition *Soak: Mumbai in an Estuary*, a study by Anuradha Mathur and Dilip da Cunha about adapting the city to increasingly frequent inundation—a project they also presented as a workshop and studio at the University of Pennsylvania.[9] I was determined that in New York, in a country where far too many resources are spent trying to deny the phenomenon of climate change rather than address it, the Museum would provide a similar platform for broad public debate. This seemed particularly important in light of the new and prominent national discussion, after the financial crisis of autumn 2008, about the role of the federal government in investing in infrastructure. Between 2008 and 2010 the federal government made a massive investment in infrastructure projects in the form of a $787 billion stimulus package, intending to address urgent needs in transportation, flood protection, and coastal management, all the while putting unemployed citizens back to work. This approach has since been criticized from all points on the political spectrum, from those who, like economist and *New York Times* columnist Paul Krugman, argue that the amount was too small and the investment too dispersed, to those who argue for budgetary austerity rather than neo-Keynesian stimulus. The package was a noble effort, but it embodied inherent conflicts and paradoxes. Not least is the typical atomization of projects by congressional district and the urgency to begin construction immediately; the latter requirement necessarily shortchanged the study of new solutions to vital problems—study that predictions of unprecedented climate change make imperative. "Shovel ready" and innovation simply do not conjugate easily and certainly not in the future conditional, which was the favored verb tense of the *Rising Currents* workshop and exhibition.

Tidal flooding encroaches on shops and homes in Can Tho, Vietnam, November 2008.

FEBRUARY 9, 2010

The *Rising Currents* proposals tell us that we may need to think in a completely different way about infrastructure, parks, how we live and get around, and the intersection of water and land in the cities of the twenty-first century.

—Adrian Benepe, Commissioner, New York City Department of Parks and Recreation, on the *Rising Currents* blog

Barry Bergdoll introduces the *Rising Currents* project to visitors (top), and visitors view work in progress by teams led by LTL Architects (middle) and Matthew Baird Architects (bottom), at the *Rising Currents* open house at MoMA PS1, December 12, 2009.

THE WORKSHOP

The five sites explored in *Rising Currents* are roughly equivalent to those delineated as test cases in *On the Water: Palisade Bay,* the 2007–09 study by Guy Nordenson, Catherine Seavitt, and Adam Yarinsky. *On the Water* is fundamental to our project. Catalyzed by predictions of rising sea level and other effects of climate change, it is at once a historical account of the transformation of the New York–New Jersey Upper Bay from one of the world's great natural harbors into one of its most elaborately reconfigured man-made ports, and a manual for interventions on its coastlines that would both ameliorate the effects of climate change and make the water, once again, the focal point of the city. In addition, it is an appeal to augment the usual toolbox of so-called "hard infrastructure" solutions (such as the concrete seawalls and storm barriers preferred by the US Army Corps of Engineers) with a whole range of soft infrastructure solutions—artificial islands, wind farms, oyster beds, absorptive wetlands (including berms and sunken capture areas)—and the possibility of simply allowing some areas to submerge under an occasional *acqua alta,* as in Venice: "Despite our best efforts," climate-change scientist Michael Oppenheimer declares in the preface to the study, "the city and the water remain one organism. As the sea rises and the storms intensify, the water will break down the boundary again and again. The question is whether we should build faster and harder to keep it out, or find a way to gently merge ourselves with the water once again, transforming the hard boundary into a continuum, a smooth transition, a commingling rather than a battle zone."[10]

Eager to extend this provocative question through the frame of the Museum, in 2008 I began discussing with Nordenson how *On the Water* might become an exhibition.[11] We considered asking some of the most successful Dutch designers to come to New Amsterdam to respond to the proposals in *On the Water,* maybe even in conjunction with the quatercentenary of the Hudson River, which for a season focused attention on the vital relationship of the city to its great river and harbor. In September of that year, during the previews of the 11th International Architecture Exhibition at the Venice Biennale, violent storms and high water in Venice were accompanied by the unfolding drama in the newspapers of the collapse of Lehman Brothers in New York and the turmoil it was unleashing in the world financial markets. By the end of the year, layoffs in New York architecture firms had reached alarming levels. From this set of challenging circumstances the idea of an exhibition on Nordenson, Seavitt, and Yarinsky's study began to take on new dimensions. Our conversation turned to the idea of a workshop, and to the formulation of twin goals: reconceiving rising sea level and increasing storm surges from enemies to be combated into new conditions to be designed for—from problems to opportunities—and tapping the generation of architects and designers, poised to make significant contributions, that might be lost to the profession at a moment when so many offices were experiencing a sudden loss of commissions.

In September 2009, with the support of a substantial grant from the Rockefeller Foundation, we invited some sixty educators and leading practitioners in architecture, landscape architecture, and engineering from around the country to nominate emerging design talents for a workshop based on *On the Water*'s challenges and recommendations. Nominees were to assemble teams from their offices and from the larger pool of talent available in the recession. In October, ten finalist teams were interviewed and four were selected to take up residence at MoMA PS1; their leaders are recently established practitioners, most of whom divide their time between a small-to-medium-sized office and a university school of architecture. They were joined by a team headed by Yarinsky and Stephen Cassell of Architecture Research Office (ARO) in partnership with Susannah C. Drake of dlandstudio. ARO had worked on a proposal for *On the Water,* and the firm was invited to continue and expand the work. During an intense eight weeks, punctuated by weekly reviews by me, Nordenson, Seavitt, and numerous guests, the teams—some thirty people in all—worked in a marvelous spirit of cooperation and exchange. A self-published version of *On the Water* was made available to them, while MoMA teamed up with Hatje Cantz and the Princeton University School of Architecture (all three authors teach at the university) to republish the book in time for the opening of the exhibition at MoMA.[12] Its valuable compilation and analysis of historical cartography and the hydraulic, topographic, and bathymetric features of the New York–New Jersey Upper Bay allowed the teams to grasp quickly the characteristics of their sites and turn almost immediately to design solutions.

Visitors also provided important preliminary information to the teams, notably those from the Marine Sciences Research Center at the State University of New York at Stony Brook. Six years ago, scientists at the center proposed the construction of three flood-gates for New York City—in the Narrows between Brooklyn and Staten Island, at the upper end of the East River, and in the tidal strait between New Jersey and Staten Island—a technique modeled on the Delta Works in the Netherlands and the Thames Barrier in London, both of which can be put into action to protect cities from coastal flooding. Stony Brook University has some of the most sophisticated equipment for the as-yet-imperfect science of modeling storm surges, so the scientists were able to offer the teams invaluable advice on the viability of various scenarios and design solutions. Other visitors followed in successive weeks. Some, actively involved in planning and environmental advocacy in the New York region, were invited to share their expertise or engage in conversation. Others who learned of the project asked to become involved. Amanda Burden, chair of New York's City Planning Commission and director of the Department of City Planning; Tom Wright, executive director of the Regional Plan Association; and Nordenson all gave public presentations as an orientation to the project. Observers and critics from the Port Authority of New York and New Jersey, the New York State Sea Level Rise Task Force, the New York State Department of Environmental Conservation Office of Environmental Justice, the Governors Island Preservation and Education Corporation, the New York City Mayor's Office of Long-Term Planning and Sustainability, the City Planning and Parks and Recreation departments, and the Hudson-Fulton-Champlain Quadricentennial Commission visited, responding to the teams' evolving work and absorbing the potency of the new techniques being explored. We held two open houses, in December 2009 and January 2010, to which the general public was invited to discuss the workshop's goals and hear about the work in progress.

LEFT: Visitors view work in progress by the team led by Kate Orff of SCAPE at the *Rising Currents* open house, December 12, 2009.

OPPOSITE: The *Rising Currents* exhibition at The Museum of Modern Art, New York, 2010.

RISING CURRENTS

PROJECTS FOR NEW YORK'S WATERFRONT

FOR MORE INFORMATION VISIT
MoMA.ORG/RISINGCURRENTS

The New York City Panel on Climate Change has predicted that sea levels will rise some two feet within the next fifty years; in the last year, evidence of rapidly melting polar ice has led some scientists to predict increases between four and six feet by the end of the century. More frequent storm surges are also predicted. *Rising Currents* was conceived in response to these threats. A jury of museum and design professionals chose five designers to assemble teams to study possible solutions for the region.

The teams studied five zones, including a wide variety of terrains: the heights on either side of the Verrazano Narrows Bridge, the low-lying lands of Bayonne and Jersey City, [...] and the banks of the Gowanus Canal in Brooklyn, for example. Teams worked alone and in [...] change but were not tasked with creating a master plan. They responded to the projections of [...] their visions of a resilient and vibrant waterfront do not necessarily comply with current [...] real-estate interests but are solutions of wide applicability.

The teams were asked to consider a greater deployment [...] structure instead of relying solely on the traditional, defensive infrastructure of levies, [...] barriers built by the US Army Corps of Engineers. Soft infrastructure includes restore[...] water and slowly manage sea-level change, artificial islands that attenuate waves and [...] of storm surges, and the exploitation of marine life—in particular the cleansing pot[...] New York Harbor.

In recent months similar studies have been anno[...] and wake of the 2009 Copenhagen Climate Change Summit, most notably [...], Liverpool, and Hull. The work on display here may be applicable to othe[...] levels and changed weather patterns over the course of the century. Ea[...] renderings, models, and animations. Video guides for each of the propos[...] be found next to their models on the central platform.

[...]IZED BY BARRY BERGDOLL,
[...]EF CURATOR OF ARCHITECTURE

[...] POSSIBLE BY THE ROCKEFELLER
[...]RST OF FIVE EXHIBITIONS IN
[...]NTEMPORARY ARCHITECTURE,
[...]GER

2 FT A RECENT STUDY BY THE NEW YORK CITY PANEL
ON CLIMATE CHANGE PREDICTS A SEA-LEVEL RISE
OF UP TO TWO FEET BY 2080

ABOVE: New Urban Ground.

BELOW: Model for New Urban Ground in the *Rising Currents* exhibition.

The teams based their work on the projections of climate-change effects summarized in *On the Water* and did not temper their visions by responding to existing real estate interests or current land-use regulations. They worked in collaborative interchange but were not charged with making a master plan; the aim was not to create a planning document for New York City—one that might easily enter the annals of unrealized urban plans—but rather to produce designs rich in attractive ideas that could be used elsewhere in the region or adapted to other cities around the world. I repeatedly reminded the teams of the task at hand: "Your mission is to come up with images that are so compelling they can't be forgotten and so realistic they can't be dismissed."

The proposal for Lower Manhattan by the team led by Cassell and Yarinsky of ARO and Drake of dlandstudio is typical of all the *Rising Currents* projects in being site specific while containing many ideas with far wider applicability. Drake had conceived a landscape of absorptive material for the highly polluted Gowanus Canal (declared a US Environmental Protection Agency Superfund site while the workshop was underway) in a 2008 project called Sponge Park, and the team's project for *Rising Currents*, New Urban Ground, extends that concept into a comprehensive rethinking of the texture of the coastline and the urban street.[13] Transformed through new wetlands, the coast is a complex natural instrument for filtering both tidal change and street runoff after storms, and the streets themselves are "greened" through surfacing in absorptive, open-mesh concrete tiles and a layered filtering system.

ABOVE: Site plan for Working Waterline with inset animation stills and model sections in the *Rising Currents* exhibition.

BELOW: Details of models for Working Waterline showing a cluster of glass reef components and shipping routes.

OVERLEAF: Visitors at the *Rising Currents* exhibition.

Leading a team of young architects, ecologists, and a landscape designer—plus artist consultants Mark Dion and Matthew Ritchie—Matthew Baird of Matthew Baird Architects tackled a site that includes an oil tank farm in Bayonne, New Jersey. As polluted land, it must be protected from flooding as sea level rises. A large berm is the last defense in a series of interventions proposed by the team, which includes recycled-glass "jacks" distributed in shallow coastal waters to attenuate waves, particularly during storm surges. The berm and these aquatic reefs create new recreational opportunities but do not entirely transform the site's industrial character: the oil tanks are converted into a biofuel facility, and World War II–era piers and warehouses support a recycling operation. With the melting of ice in the Arctic, shipping routes have been opened in the last few years that will undoubtedly reshape the maritime economy of the New York/New Jersey harbor; the team's proposal, Working Waterline, envisions new natural and economic ecologies for the region.

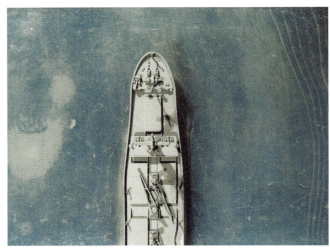

The group led by Kate Orff of SCAPE proposes a massive project of wildlife restoration. New York's waters, as Mark Kurlansky has demonstrated in his recent popular ecological history *The Big Oyster: History on the Half Shell*, were once home to numerous oyster beds, and oysters were a major part of the city's diet and economy as well as the harbor's ecology.[14] Orff's team proposes to transform the Gowanus Canal from one of the country's most polluted waterways into one of its most productive oyster hatcheries. The canal has many properties that make it an ideal site for oyster cultivation, Orff argues, and the mollusks, in turn, assist in cleaning the water. Once they are hatched, the oysters are relocated to the Bay Ridge Flats, south of Governors Island, where they create a wave-attenuating reef and a new natural aquatic park, protect the adjacent shoreline, and stimulate the growth of other marine life. Planning here is not simply static design but the implementation and exploitation of dynamic natural systems.

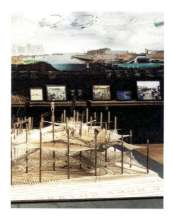

OPPOSITE: Rendering of Oyster-tecture in the *Rising Currents* exhibition (top) with model of oyster reef (bottom).

TOP: Detail of New Aqueous City showing man-made islands connected by barriers that inflate in the event of storm-surge flooding.

BOTTOM: New Aqueous City installation in the *Rising Currents* exhibition.

The proposal by the team led by Eric Bunge and Mimi Hoang of nARCHITECTS introduces a network of artificial islands into the harbor, just north of the Verrazano-Narrows Bridge, the nodal points in a system of submerged inflatable barriers that will minimize storm surges. This is not a new technology; but here it is deployed as a component of the team's vision of a "new aqueous city"—a form of urbanism in which the city extends into the water, and water enters the city. An ever-growing population is accommodated by aqueous neighborhoods featuring suspended housing, wave-attenuating piers, and service by a new generation of biogas ferries and a tramway. Land neighborhoods are punctuated by basins and culverts that absorb storm runoff and function as parks in dry weather.

The team led by Paul Lewis, Marc Tsurumaki, and David J. Lewis of LTL Architects created some of the most beautiful images to result from the workshop. Their low-lying site—Liberty State Park—is man-made; it did not exist 150 years ago, and if no intervention is made it will not exist in large measure a century from now. The team stepped back in time to imagine the harbor as a place of blurred lines between land and sea.[15] They propose to cut into the existing landfill and redeploy it to achieve a varied topography on the flat site, a crenellated landscape of jagged fingers that, by lengthening the coastline manyfold, allows it to attenuate waves and serve as a natural filter of tidewater. The new topography of Water Proving Ground is zoned for a range of urban functions, from leisure and recreation to aquaculture and commerce, all placed on the site in relationship to the degree of protection the elevation offers from flooding.

The five projects are highly individual—indeed, one of our goals was to encourage an artistic signature in infrastructure design—but they share a number of features, which in sum illustrate the lessons of *Rising Currents*. Throughout the proposals, the benefits of a more varied seafloor are espoused, in artificial and natural reefs and islands built of materials ranging from recycled glass to oysters to conventional landfill. They embrace a natural transition between water and land, introducing absorptive wetlands both to ameliorate changes in sea level and support recreational facilities and restored natural habitats, and they propose flexible forms of interpenetration of water and land, extending the city into the sea, and the sea into the city. Nature itself is incorporated into the

TOP: Detail of Water Proving Ground showing an amphitheater adjacent to Liberty Island that operates as a venue for outdoor concerts.

BOTTOM: Detail of projection model for Water Proving Ground showing predicted storm-surge flooding.

OVERLEAF: Project models and site plans in the *Rising Currents* exhibition.

design vocabulary of architecture, a trend that has been growing in recent years with the rapprochement between architecture and landscape design—a blurring of professional boundaries parallel to the continuity proposed in *On the Water* and *Rising Currents* between topography and bathymetry, land and sea.

The workshop's experimental approach to design was paralleled in the planning of the exhibition. In review and critique sessions during the weeks leading up to the show, comments on the projects by me, Nordenson, and Seavitt (who were actively engaged as critics) moved seamlessly into discussions of graphic and modeled depictions of their components and the strategy for exhibition. The installation design was the collective work of the teams, of me as curator, and of MoMA exhibition designer and production manager Lana Hum and exhibition graphic designer Hsien-yin Ingrid Chou. Rarely in exhibition preparation are the designers of the installation and the graphic scheme involved in conversations during the making of the work itself, but in our process they were key participants. A dedicated website within MoMA.org was developed for the project, and during the workshop the teams and many of the visiting critics posted regular process and progress reports, reactions, and impressions.

When the exhibition had been up for several weeks, we realized how catalytic the whole experiment had been. The gallery was continually filled with visitors engaged in reading the wall texts, studying the designs, and taking in the experience of the architecture pinup through video interviews with the team leaders. During the show the website hosted a series of guest editorials about the project by observers from outside the process: Adrian Benepe, commissioner of the New York City Department of Parks and Recreation; Leslie Koch, executive director of the Governors Island Preservation and Education Corporation; Adriaan Geuze, an architect developing a park on Governors Island; and many others. The site was an ongoing forum for reactions, responses, and dialogue among members of the general public, visiting architects, and Museum visitors in the galleries, where two computers were provided for access.

Continual invitations to me, to Nordenson, and to team members to lecture on *Rising Currents,* even after the exhibition had closed, convinced us that it would be desirable to publish the projects, making them available to designers and students embarking on workshops on related themes and public officials planning for more resilient cities. It is our sincere hope that these projects will continue to contribute to a discussion of the role design has to play in meeting the challenges posed by climate change. We also hope that these five projects will be launching pads for other studies, studios in architecture schools, workshops in city planning offices, and debates in which public policy and design will interact in productive ways. Both the workshop and the exhibition are responses to the very real challenges delineated in *On the Water*. Their successes in generating new design ideas and new conversations are reasons to believe that New York and other cities around the world can transform themselves in productive, positive ways—for land, sea, and citizens alike—in response to environmental challenges larger, perhaps, than any faced before.

FEBRUARY 9, 2010

From the Parks point of view, the proposals represent some innovative ways to create new realms of public space, places that are not traditional parks, but rather are flexible zones of water and land and plants and animals. We currently tend to look at parks as distinct from other urban forms, with fences, walls, planted buffers—different vocabularies of building materials. While each team has proposed concepts very different from the others, they all redefine the interaction of streets, parks, seawalls, canals, piers, and even the harbor itself.

—Adrian Benepe, Commissioner, New York City Department of Parks and Recreation, on the *Rising Currents* blog

FEBRUARY 17, 2010

The work of the five teams at P.S.1 illustrates that climate change will require us to alter the way we behave as individuals, build and operate infrastructure, design buildings, utilize land, manage natural resources, make investments, and plan for the future. Their work emphasizes innovative strategies that enhance our built environment while embracing the natural environment—even as it changes around us.

—Adam Freed, Deputy Director, Mayor's Office of Long-Term Planning and Sustainability, New York, on the *Rising Currents* blog

NOTES

1. The venue was made available through the program Free Space, an ongoing collaboration between MoMA PS1, artists, and nonprofit arts institutions initiated in 2009. Participating artists and groups are invited to use MoMA PS1's gallery space for research and development in exchange for a public performance, event, or exhibition. The goal of the program is to support the New York arts community during the economic downturn.

2. *Modern Architecture: International Exhibition*, organized by Henry-Russell Hitchcock and Philip Johnson, was on view at The Museum of Modern Art, New York, February 9–March 23, 1932. *Housing Exhibition of the City of New York*, organized by G. Lyman Paine, Jr., was on view at MoMA October 15–November 7, 1934. On the 1932 exhibition, see Terence Riley, *The International Style: Exhibition 15 and the Museum of Modern Art* (New York: Rizzoli and Columbia Books on Architecture, 1992).

3. *The New City: Architecture and Urban Renewal*, organized by Arthur Drexler, was on view at The Museum of Modern Art, New York, January 24–March 13, 1967. See Elizabeth Kassler, Sidney J. Frigand, and Arthur Drexler, *The New City: Architecture and Urban Renewal* (New York: The Museum of Modern Art, 1967).

4. *Home Delivery: Fabricating the Modern Dwelling*, organized by Barry Bergdoll and Peter Christensen, was on view at The Museum of Modern Art, New York, July 20–October 20, 2008. See Bergdoll and Christensen, *Home Delivery: Fabricating the Modern Dwelling* (New York: The Museum of Modern Art, 2008).

5. For more information about this and other aspects of *Home Delivery*, see Bergdoll, "Plein-air Prefab," *The Skira Yearbook of World Architecture, 2007–2008* (Milan: Skira, 2008), 88–89.

6. Seth Mydans, "Vietnam Finds Itself Vulnerable if Sea Rises," *New York Times*, September 24, 2009, http://www.nytimes.com/2009/09/24/world/asia/24delta.html.

7. "Developing Countries and Global Warming: A Bad Climate for Development," *The Economist*, September 17, 2009, http://www.economist.com/node/14447171.

8. *Klima X*, a collaboration among the host museum, The International Polar Year (IPY), the Centre for International Climate and Environmental Research, Oslo (CICERO), The Norwegian University of Science and Technology (NTNU), Trondheim, The Norwegian Meteorological Institute (DNMI), The University Centre of Svalbard (UNIS), The University of Oslo (UoO), Statistics Norway (SSB), World Wide Fund for Nature (WWF), Bellona Foundation, Institute for Energy Technology (IFE), and The Norwegian Oil Industry Association (OLF), was on view at the Norwegian National Museum of Science, Technology, and Medicine, Oslo, 2007–09.

9. *Soak: Mumbai in an Estuary*, organized by Anuradha Mathur and Dilip da Cunha, was on view at the National Gallery of Modern Art, Mumbai, June 23–August 23, 2009. See Mathur and da Cunha, *Soak: Mumbai in an Estuary* (Calcutta: Rupa Co., 2009).

10. Michael Oppenheimer, preface to Guy Nordenson, Catherine Seavitt, and Adam Yarinsky, *On the Water: Palisade Bay* (Berlin: Hatje Cantz/The Museum of Modern Art, 2010), 10.

11. For more information on the process, see Bergdoll, afterword to Nordenson et al., *On the Water*, 301–303.

12. This is Nordenson et al., *On the Water*. See note 10.

13. For more information about Sponge Park, see the project website at http://www.spongepark.org/.

14. Mark Kurlansky, *The Big Oyster: History on the Half Shell* (New York: Ballantine Books, 2006).

15. The island of Manhattan as Henry Hudson found it in 1609 is brought vividly to life by Eric W. Sanderson in *Mannahatta: A Natural History of New York City* (New York: Abrams, 2009).

CLIMATE CHANGE AND WORLD CITIES

Michael Oppenheimer

Cities—those vibrant multicultural platforms for interaction, industry, and ingenuity, where the worst and best humanity has to offer are often on display in close proximity—are caught in a pincer. A seemingly inexorable emigration of people from rural to urban areas is accelerating. Urban population around the globe is projected to grow by 1.6 billion by 2030 (due to migration and births), while the rural population shrinks by 28 million.[1] In China alone, about forty thousand people per day make the trek from country to city, and most will never return.[2] However, just as the total population of cities and towns exceeds that of rural areas for the first time in human history, cities face a new threat: climate change.

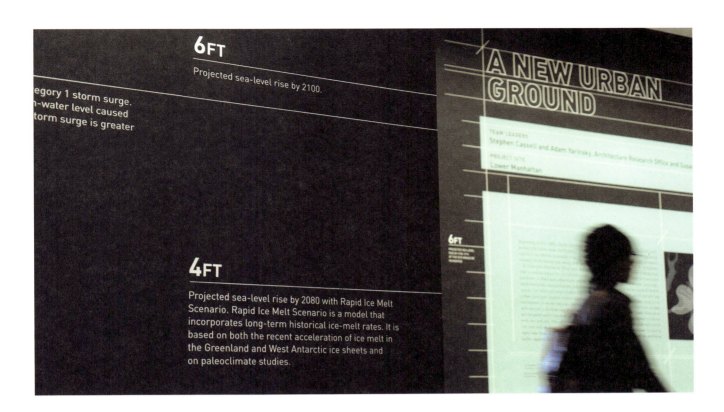

Our atmosphere is transparent to the sunlight that provides almost all the heat available at Earth's surface. As the surface warms, it radiates heat back into space. But the atmosphere contains heat-trapping "greenhouse" gases, such as carbon dioxide and water vapor, which act like a blanket, absorbing some of the outgoing heat, warming the surface further, and establishing the equable climate that nurtures life as we know it. Unfortunately, humans are upsetting this long-established balancing act. We draw our energy for electric power plants, cars, and factories largely from the combustion of fossil fuels: coal, oil, and natural gas. The carbon dioxide and other gases emitted in the process are thickening the atmospheric blanket. Earth is experiencing a global warming.

This much is fact. Data from a network of thermometers, supplemented by recent satellite measurements, has produced a reliable 150-year record that reveals a spatial pattern of warming bearing the unique signature of the greenhouse effect.[3] Simultaneously, sea level is rising for two reasons: the warming of the ocean is measurable down to thousands of feet, and ocean water, like any fluid, expands when it is heated; and mountaintops and polar lands are covered with ice, which is warming as well. What does ice do when it warms? It eventually melts. Where does that meltwater go? Eventually, it flows into the ocean, further raising the sea level. Earth has warmed by about 1.4 degrees Fahrenheit (0.8°C) over the 150-year period of measurement. Additional warming is inevitable because the oceans are so big that they warm up slowly, lagging behind the temperature dictated by gases already emitted. Sea level has already risen about 7 inches (15–20 cm). Projections of sea level rise over this century depend on how much additional gas we emit before reining in the problem. Estimates run as high as 3 feet (about 1 m) or more (enough to permanently inundate a 300-foot width of Atlantic coast beach) but are very uncertain due to our inability to accurately predict the response of the polar ice sheets to warming.[4] In addition, coastal storms episodically drive the ocean inland, temporarily flooding large areas of land and then withdrawing again. In the future, storms of the same intensity as today's will be pushing a sea that starts out at a higher level. As a result, water will reach further inland, flooding larger areas. Abandonment of episodically flooded lands could occur long before permanent inundation.

Most of humanity lives near or at a coast, and many people are clustered in cities. A virtue of cities is that they can accommodate large numbers of residents in close proximity to resources, such as harbors, where they can work efficiently, moving goods and services around the world. But cities accomplish this task by taming the coastline, replacing beach and wetland with cement and building right up to the edge of the water. Scientists have studied forty large river deltas, and most are a functional hodgepodge of agricultural land enriched by fluvial sediment, densely concentrated populations, and megacities with expensive infrastructure, a high level of economic activity, and an uneven distribution of wealth. About five hundred million of us live on those deltas, in cities including New Orleans, Amsterdam, Dacca, and Shanghai.[5] But that's not the end of the story. Add to this number the hundreds of millions living in other urbanized coastal zones, not situated on deltas but still at sea level in the tidal zone, like New York, Miami, Washington, D.C., London, Sydney, Bangkok, and Mumbai.

That their relatively inflexible infrastructure makes them particularly vulnerable to sea level rise is but one of several characteristics unique to urban areas that have become problematic in a warming world. Most notable is the phenomenon of the urban heat island. The high density of energy-generating activities, a preponderance of dark surfaces (which absorb heat readily), concrete (which releases the heat of the day only slowly at night), and paving (which shuts off natural sources of moisture whose evaporation would moderate high temperature) are among the factors keeping urban temperatures elevated above those of the surrounding countryside, particularly at night. As areas of the Middle East and Southwest Asia urbanize over this century, nighttime urban temperatures in those regions could increase by as much as 10 degrees Fahrenheit (6°C) over surrounding rural areas.[6]

In North America and Europe, urbanization may have largely run its course, but global warming will further raise temperatures in urban heat islands. It is well-known from studies of mortality rates in heat waves that high nighttime temperatures are particularly deadly, because it is at night that the body's metabolism recovers from the stresses of the day. Even a short string of nights in which temperatures stay above 80 degrees Fahrenheit (27°C) can be highly problematic. Deadly heat waves are fairly common in tropical developing countries like India. But even highly developed northern countries are not immune. Approximately forty thousand deaths across Western Europe were attributed to the direct and indirect effects of a suffocating heat wave that struck in August 2003. That heat wave was a once-in-a-thousand-years event: that is, in any one year, it had about a 0.1 percent chance of occurring. But computer models that project global climate change show that greenhouse gas buildup could make such events yearly occurrences by the end of this century. The risk of heat-related deaths would be compounded in urban heat islands.[7]

Freshwater flooding, resulting from heavy rainstorms, is another issue for urban areas. Global warming makes the atmosphere wetter overall, because as the surface of the sea warms, the evaporation of water into the atmosphere increases. What goes up must come down, and in the case of this extra water vapor it comes down mostly at times when rain would occur anyway. In other words, the extra water makes existing rainstorms yet more intense. In the northeastern United States, storms delivering over 2 inches (5 cm) of precipitation in twenty-four hours are relatively rare, occurring only a few times per year. But the frequency of such events has increased over the past century, and the aforementioned computer models project an even greater increase in the coming decades. Here again, the rigid structure of cities works against them. Under natural circumstances, water is absorbed and drained away by soil and vegetation, which moderates the potential for damaging floods. But urban areas have largely been paved over, and water can't drain away harmlessly. Instead, it seeks low points on the surface, like a dip in the pavement under a highway overpass or the basement of a house. The result is costly damage and sometimes loss of life.

An emerging area of interest is the connection between global warming and human migration. Case studies from Burkina Faso, Nepal, Mexico, and the United States (including the Dust Bowl) demonstrate that people often move when climate conditions become unfavorable to agriculture.[8] All other things being equal, under unfavorable climatic conditions a farmer in Mexico might decide that prospects look brighter across the border. But once the farmer emigrates, he is unlikely to take up farming. More likely, he will move to a city and pursue other options. So an indirect consequence of global warming may be an acceleration of the trend toward urbanization already underway.

Let's step back and consider the picture we have painted. Urban areas are already bursting at the seams as a result of a flow of migrants from rural areas. This is a world-wide phenomenon, and there is no reason to believe it will reverse (although particular circumstances could favor a return flow in specific areas); furthermore, we can expect global warming to accelerate this trend. Urban areas currently accommodate these migrants, for better or worse, and adapt to the flow, although some of these adaptations, like slums, may leave the inhabitants worse off than they were in the situation they left. At the same time, the risks to human well-being from heat waves, sea level rise, episodic storms, and flooding are expected to increase over time, and as more and more people move to urban areas these risks will be compounded.

Even the most forward-looking design can only ameliorate, not solve, the problem, since it is not likely that we will ever be able to predict the future with sufficient accuracy and far enough in advance to completely implement the necessary approaches. And if the climate warms as rapidly as some projections suggest, we won't be able to imple-ment either the old or the newer approaches fast enough to meet the challenge. This brings us to what must be the central element of any effective program to solve the climate problem: reducing the emissions that are causing the warming. Given the rugged road faced by domestic climate legislation and negotiations such as those at the 2009 United Nations Climate Change Conference in Copenhagen, it is fair to ask if there is any realistic prospect for emissions reductions that would make a dent in the warming trend. There are credible opinions on both sides of the question, but some recent developments suggest that we are muddling toward a lower-emissions world.

The United States is often painted as a renegade on emissions-reduction efforts due to its 2001 withdrawal from the Kyoto Protocol global warming treaty, but through a combination of intentional and inadvertent actions it has reduced its total greenhouse gas emissions slightly over the past decade, countering rather than continuing the upward march that has characterized previous decades. The plateauing of emissions was well underway before the 2008 financial crisis struck.[9] Even without comprehensive federal legislation, automotive fuel economy and appliance efficiency standards have been tightened by executive action (both approaches reduce energy use and, therefore, the burning of fossil fuel), states have implemented greenhouse gas emissions limits on electric power plants and other sources, and individual cities (many realizing the looming problems outlined above) have begun to plan farsighted programs to reconfigure new development and, to some extent, renovate existing systems to increase efficiency and reduce overall emissions. ICLEI—Local Governments for Sustainability (formerly the International Council for Local Environmental Initiatives) has aided in this by facilitating pilot projects and providing a vehicle for information sharing.

When the United States dropped out of the Kyoto Protocol, the European Union pressed forward, and its member states are more or less on track to meet their obligations. Of course, such progress was facilitated by the financial crisis dampening energy demand,

6FT

Projected sea-level rise by 2100.

5FT 8IN

Projected sea-level rise with a category 1 storm surge.
A storm surge is a short-term high-water level caused
by a weather event. A category 3 storm surge is greater
than a category 1 storm surge.

4F

Pr
So
i

2FT

Projected sea-level

but a quick tour around Germany, the Netherlands, and Denmark, among other European countries, shows that wind and solar energy have made a significant dent in the electricity generation market; wind provides about twenty percent of Denmark's electricity and eight percent of Germany's.[10] We have gotten two key advances out of the much-maligned Protocol: a large amount of learning about how to organize to fight global warming, including an emissions-permit trading system (a system that sets a price on pollution, an idea the European Union picked up from the United States before the latter dropped out of the Protocol) as well as some meaningful emissions cuts.

Finally, China has its own ideas about the climate issue and, in contrast to its stance over most of the past twenty years, these go well beyond hoping climate worries will evaporate. China burns so much coal that even though it sits atop about thirteen percent of the global reserves, it imports a significant amount from Australia.[11] Its concern over air pollution has fueled a search for alternatives to coal, and the government envisions an economic advantage from cornering various components of the global clean-energy market (it is now the leader in solar cell and wind turbine production). At the same time, its government and scientists take projections of rising sea level seriously; one especially vulnerable area is China's vast coastal zone, where densely populated urban areas, including Shanghai, sit right by the sea, subject to all the risk and uncertainty noted above. One result of this sense of both threat and opportunity is China's willingness to publicly set a target for its domestic emissions limitation through 2020: a forty to forty-five percent cut per unit of gross domestic product, which it intends to enforce as a key part of an energy policy designed to maintain a rapidly growing domestic economy.[12] This and similar commitments by Brazil and several other developing countries were the most important outcomes of the Copenhagen conference, developments that were maintained at the 2010 United Nations Climate Change Summit in Cancun.

If such efforts to reduce greenhouse gas emissions fall short, the opportunity to avoid a dangerous climate change and corresponding sea level rise would disappear. Then our cities would face an unpleasant, difficult, and calamitous future. And given the inevitability of some further warming even if we cut emissions sharply, plus the uncertainty of predictions about precisely how much change is in the offing, we must plan to adapt to a warmer climate no matter what. One possible response is to pursue what have been the standard approaches: if vulnerable people are at risk of heat-related deaths, then make sure they have access to air-conditioning; if heavy rainstorms threaten more and more flooding, then build more storm sewers and lay more drainpipes; as sea level rises, harden the coast more and more, build more seawalls and storm protection (like the Thames Barrier), pile more sand along it (as the Netherlands is doing). These methods work, at least in part, but they are costly, they often simply displace the problem (a standard strategy for urban areas), and they almost always do severe damage to what's left of the natural environment in the vicinity. Finally, often being literally set in stone, such "hard infrastructure" is dependent on a stable climate and sea level, and these are two options we simply cannot count on any longer.

Putting more thought now into how we want our cities to evolve is a far wiser course than simply doing it the old-fashioned way. Other options are available, and we can see the stirrings of a different future in small-scale experiments taking place in cities around the world. Roofs painted a glistening silvery color reflect sunlight, reducing the impact of warming. Floating houses soften the blow from coastal flooding. Semipermeable hardened surfaces allow water to seep through to the ground instead of channeling it to a low point, creating a flood. And as the projects described in this book demonstrate, there are abundant options for softening the interface between urban land and sea, turning a battle zone into an area of peaceful transition. Implementing the new and the old in a sensible combination, while moving promptly to reduce emissions, will provide our cities with their best chance to thrive.

HIGH STAKES: SOFT INFRASTRUCTURE FOR THE RISING SEAS **Guy Nordenson and Catherine Seavitt**

At the end of a hundred leagues we found a very agreeable
location situated within two prominent hills, in the midst
of which flowed to the sea a very great river, which was deep
at the mouth.
—Giovanni da Verrazano, 1524 CE

Ego sum, pleno quem flumine cernis
stringentem ripas et pinguia culta secantem,
caeruleus Thybris, caelo gratissimus amnis.
Hic mihi magna domus, celsis caput urbibus exit.
—Virgil, 29–19 BCE[1]

INONDAZIONE

During a flood, a city is transformed. The displacement of a volume of water—the rise of a purely horizontal liquid datum along the vertical axis—creates radical planar reconfigurations. Perhaps the foremost example of such volatility is the city of Rome, which is marked extensively by the historically relentless floods of the Tiber River. Throughout the city, markers and hydrometers register the heights of extreme floods. Since the construction of the *muraglioni*, or embankment walls, a massive urban infrastructure project built between 1876 and 1910 in response to the severe flood of 1870, the urban course of the Tiber has been canalized into a uniform channel 328 feet (100 m) wide. The city has since been spared extensive flooding. Yet these vertical walls, rising to 39 feet (12 m) above sea level, have severed the city from the river. The *muraglioni* visually and physically depress the water below the level of inhabitation. Only during extreme flood events does the water rise high enough to be seen from the *Lungotevere*, the roads running parallel to the top of the floodwalls, as it did in December 2008. The flood deposited thousands of colored plastic bags (carried downstream by the current) in the branches of the trees growing along the river's edge at the base of the walls; the bags remained, flood markers of the new millennium, when the waters receded.

ABOVE: The Tiber River, shortly before the construction of the modern embankment walls. Here, the city touches the water. Alessandro Specchi's eighteenth-century baroque Porto di Ripetta is visible at the center of the image just before the river's bend. It was destroyed to make room for the embankment walls.

RIGHT: Stretch of the Tiber River above the Ponte Garibaldi after the implementation of the embankment walls, showing the sectional displacement of the city from its river.

Alternately, Venice is a city whose urban spaces are still radically transformed during periods of *acqua alta*, when the exceptionally high tidal waters of the Adriatic Sea enter the Venetian Lagoon. Elevated wooden platforms are then strategically placed throughout the city, creating new and specific pathways of movement. During the *acqua alta* of December 2008, Venice's most significant flood of the last twenty-two years, the waters rose almost 5 feet (more than 1.5 m). And while the city continues to respectfully engrave the high-water marks onto the venerable marble walls of the *Ca' Farsetti*, Venice's city hall, it is also undertaking its own massive infrastructural scheme, the MOSE project, whose acronym derives from the Italian phrase for "experimental electromechanical module." This controversial defense system of seventy-nine mobile floodgates is intended to isolate the Adriatic Sea from the city during high-tide events by rising to block the three entrances to the lagoon. It is not clear that the project, initiated in the 1970s, has accounted for predicted sea level rise due to global climate change, nor if the environmental consequences for the Venetian Lagoon are sufficiently understood.

The movement of water along a vertical scale draws attention to the subtle configurations of topography and the consequential horizontal extent of flooding. During a flood, the vertical section gives rise to new formations and understandings of a city. Today, flooding has become synonymous with the impact of global sea level rise, and the threat of rising waters has taken on a new sense of urgency. Studying the planar transformation that takes place during high-water events is an opportunity to reinvent and redesign the twenty-first-century city and consider new notions of urban and ecological development.

ON THE WATER

Our research and design study *On the Water: Palisade Bay* (begun 2007) served as the basis and backstory for the development of The Museum of Modern Art's *Rising Currents* workshop and exhibition.[2] Our research led us to question both the notion and the effectiveness of "hard infrastructure," as exemplified by seawalls and storm-surge barriers; these reduce the zone of floodwater absorption to a singular line in plan and a singular wall in section. Instead, the waterfront would best be conceived as a dynamic limit moving across a gradient. We have proposed the development of a new approach toward flooding that we call "soft infrastructure"—a collection of multiple and iterative strategies that buffer or absorb flooding. These strategies operate at the merged surface of the land's topography and the water's bathymetry—the shallow flats below the water—envisioning the water's edge as a fluid and temporal limit between the water and the land. And we respectfully accept some degree of flooding, as did the Romans for over 2,500 years.

On the Water: Palisade Bay was funded by the 2007 Latrobe Prize (named for architect Benjamin Henry Latrobe), a biennial grant awarded by the College of Fellows of The American Institute of Architects for collaborative research leading to the advancement of the profession.[3] The work reflects the initiative of a group of engineers, architects, landscape architects, and planners who collaborated to imagine the transformation of the New York–New Jersey Upper Bay in the face of certain climate change and sea level rise. Our area of study is framed by the Bayonne Bridge at the western edge of the Kill Van Kull (the tidal strait separating Staten Island and Bayonne), the Holland Tunnel and the Manhattan Bridge at the north, and the Verrazano-Narrows Bridge at the south. The surface area of the Upper Bay is approximately 20 square miles (52 km²), and it measures almost 4 miles (6.4 km) across at its widest point. We chose the Upper Bay as the site for this proposal not only because of the massive impact that sea level rise and potential storm surges from hurricanes would have on this densely populated region, but also because of its capacity to be transformed into an urban center for the region. This center would be based on shared ecological and physical boundaries rather than the arbitrary lines of political districting. We imagine the Upper Bay as a kind of Central Park for the whole region, a recentering of the city away from Manhattan to the boroughs and adjoining New Jersey counties. We envision the bay as a common ground, a site that could represent to the region what the Bacino di San Marco is to Venice—a meeting place and crossroads on the water.

Sea level rise will affect infrastructures, environments, and coastal communities around the world. By 2050, it is likely that the mean sea level in the New York/New Jersey area will rise between 6 inches and 2 feet (15–61 cm) as a result of warming oceans. Recent scientific research on the melting of the Greenland and Antarctic ice caps indicates that the relative sea level in the area could rise up to 3 feet (91 cm) by 2080.[4] Twenty million people live within 50 miles (80.5 km) of the Upper Bay, and an increase of almost one million more residents is expected by 2030. In addition, the waters of the harbor itself are home to a rich but fragile estuarine ecosystem. Both the

Venice's Piazza San Marco with the Doge's Palace under the *acqua alta* of December 1, 2008. This was the city's most significant flood in twenty-two years, with the waters rising 5 feet (1.52 m).

built and the natural elements of this tenuous relationship will be radically affected by global climate change, sea level rise, and their consequences.

Yet sea level rise is just the static aspect of climate change. The dynamic aspect derives from the depth and extent of flooding produced by storm surges. Because of higher global and local water level, it is likely that the frequency and extent of flood damage due to severe storms—hurricanes and nor'easters—will increase dramatically. What is currently considered a 100-year storm flood will recur every 19 to 68 years, and a 500-year storm flood may recur closer to every 100 years.[5] Furthermore, higher ocean temperatures could increase the frequency and severity of hurricanes and thus the chance of extreme storm surges.[6] With a Category 3 hurricane, storm surges could reach up to 24 feet (7.3 m) in the New York/New Jersey area.[7]

The hazards posed by climate change, sea level rise, and severe storm surges make it imperative that we study the adaptive design of coastal cities. The conventional response to flooding in recent history has been hard engineering—fortifying the coastal infrastructure with seawalls and bulkheads to protect real estate, at the expense of natural tidal wetlands and ecosystems. This approach has proven environmentally damaging, unsustainable, and often ineffective. The failure of levees and other coastal

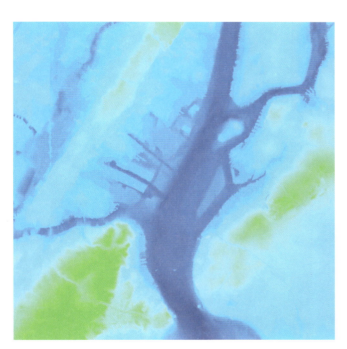

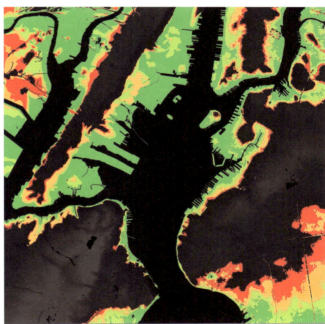

ABOVE: Bathymetric model of the Upper Bay, indicating the deepest areas in dark blue. Note the deep Verrazano Narrows, the shallow Jersey Flats to the west, the Bay Ridge Flats to the east, and the straight dredged shipping channels cutting through the Jersey Flats.

RIGHT: Inundation analysis showing sea, lake, and overland surges from hurricanes (SLOSH). Inundation from a Category 1 hurricane is indicated in dark green, Category 2 in light green, Category 3 in orange, and Category 4 in red. Dataset by the National Oceanic and Atmospheric Administration (NOAA), National Hurricane Center.

protection structures confronted by Hurricane Katrina in 2005 is a dramatic example of infrastructural inadequacy. A core premise of our research and proposal is the transformation of hard engineering practices into soft infrastructural development.

Significant research into the risks of climate change in the New York/New Jersey area has led to several proposed solutions to the problem—most notably a system of four storm-surge barriers.[8] But the shortcomings of such conventional systems should provoke a comprehensive reconsideration of coastal planning. It is time for a new approach that is sustainable from an environmental, technical, and economic standpoint, and that also has the potential to improve the quality of urban life.

PALISADE BAY

The word "palisade" frames the argument of our proposal for the Upper Bay of New York and New Jersey. The term refers to plant ecology at a cellular level (the palisade cell), geological formations (the palisade sill), and man-made fortifications (the palisade fence). Palisade derives from the Latin *palus*, meaning "stake" and, by extension, "boundary." The possibility of creating porous boundaries across politically staked borders and along the edge of water and land deeply influences this research and our design proposal.

Our Palisade Bay proposal involves more than the invention of an adaptive strategy to address sea level rise and a protective approach to flooding and storm surges. It is equally focused on developing urban place, enriching estuarine health, diversifying habitat, and transforming our understanding of the dynamic force of water in the urban condition. The water of the Upper Bay might again be seen as fluid, entering the city and retreating, giving residents a sense of tidal variation and the transformations that might occur with controlled flooding. We developed ideas for both the fresh (rainwater and rivers) and the marine (saline and tidal) components of the estuarine mix, harnessing each for appropriate uses.

We propose three adaptive strategies to transform the physical characteristics of the Upper Bay, reduce flood risk from both sea level rise and storm surges, and challenge current development strategies for water, land, and shelter:

> Create an archipelago of islands, shoals, and reefs in the Upper Bay to reduce the impact of storm-induced wave energy as well as improve the ecology of the estuarine environment. The bathymetrics of the bay will be modified, but current shipping channels will be maintained. We are exploring the possibility of harnessing wind and waves to produce energy.

> Create a soft but resilient thickened coastline edge, combining tidal marshes, public parks, and finger piers and inland slips for recreation and possible development, and determine where to selectively place protective seawalls.

> Create flexible and democratic zoning formulas for coastal development that evolve in response to climate change and storms to increase community welfare and resilience to natural disasters.

Together, these three strategies—on the water, on the coast, and in the community— form a radical proposal to transform the Upper Bay into the central focus of the region. The Upper Bay has the potential to become an ecologically sound archipelago park, a place that will be to the New York/New Jersey region in the twenty-first century what Central Park was to Manhattan in the late nineteenth century.

EDGES, FLATS, AND AQUACULTURE

A principal hypothesis of this research is that a softer shoreline—a more gradual transition from land to water—creates a more resilient edge, better able to contend with both sea level rise and increased storm-surge flooding. Transforming this edge— thickening it from the solid line of the seawall to the mucky width of tidal wetlands, restoring a fringe of piers and slips, and building a protective archipelago of islands

ABOVE: Details of the Palisade Bay proposal: an archipelago of caisson islands, seen from the Staten Island ferry terminal (top), retired subway cars transformed into underwater reefs near Liberty State Park, Jersey City (middle), and a proposed archipelago of island formations and the reshaped gradient coastline at the tip of Lower Manhattan, incorporating parks, wetlands, and a shifted seawall (bottom). Latrobe Research Team

RIGHT: Preliminary Palisade Bay master plan design strategies including wetlands, windmills, reefs, oyster beds, island fields, extended piers, detached piers, and extracted slips. Latrobe Research Team

and reefs—is central to our proposal. This broadened gradient edge would offer a buffer zone of breakwaters and relieving structures during storm surges and floods. A thickened edge, graded as a tidal wetland terrace, would also provide new habitat, improving the health of the estuarine ecosystem.

In addition to a transformation of the edge, we propose an intervention into the flats of Palisade Bay. While maintaining active shipping channels, we would restore the shoals, anchorages, and oyster beds of the bay's original bathymetrics, particularly at the Jersey City and Red Hook shores. Our scheme for a matrixlike field of caisson islands—an archipelago of shoals, oyster beds, artificial barrier reefs, and low islands—would transform the bathymetrics of the Upper Bay, acting as a breakwater and diminishing wave action and thus the extent of storm-surge flooding. In addition, this field would create a nature preserve on the water, diversifying habitat and enhancing the bay ecology.

Lastly, we envision the water of the Upper Bay as productive. Soft infrastructure would allow us to mitigate the effects of combined sewage overflow, and potentially collect and filter storm-water runoff to be used as freshwater irrigation for crops along the coastline. It would introduce mollusks, such as mussels and oysters, to clean and filter the polluted waters, with the hope that the bay will become so clean that it can once again support a thriving aquaculture. And ultimately it would also harness the energy of the region's water and air with tidal and wind turbines, perhaps creating green biofuel from algae farms. When its rich ecosystem is brought back to health through soft infrastructure, the Upper Bay, we predict, will teem with life—not just a human population, but also mollusks, crustaceans, fish, birds, phytoplankton, and marsh grasses and other plants.

The Palisade Bay proposal seeks not merely to protect the New York/New Jersey region from sea level rise and storm-surge flooding, but also to reconceptualize the relationship between adaptive infrastructure and ecology in the twenty-first-century waterfront city. It is an attempt to reconcile environmental stewardship and infrastructural development. With climate change as our catalyst, we aspire to develop a new and versatile system of coastal planning; to enrich the ecosystem, habitat, and health of the urban estuary; and to create new methods of making the water a vital urban place.

REFLECTIONS ON *RISING CURRENTS*

The combination workshop and exhibition that was *Rising Currents* brought together five teams of architects, landscape architects, engineers, ecologists, and artists to envision projects on five delineated sites within Palisade Bay. The workshop and exhibition also served as forums for discussions with government officials, both local and federal, community groups, and individual members of the public. These interactions helped shape and refine the projects and influence policy.

In residence at MoMA PS1, the five teams developed their visions for five discrete zones of the Upper Bay waterfront. Our etymological *palisade* triad (ecology, geology, and fortification) appears in each proposal to varying degrees: in Oyster-tecture's use of the shallow bathymetry of the Gowanus Canal/Bay Ridge Flats and fuzzy rope as materials to reseed oyster reefs and attenuate wave energy; in Working Waterline's harnessing of cellular ecology in disused Bayonne oil tanks, creating biofuel from algae fed by wastewater; in Water Proving Ground's subtle topographic shifts at Liberty State Park, resulting in programmatic "petri dishes" of protected and productive areas; in New Urban Ground's protective strategy for Lower Manhattan, transforming the underbelly of the hard streets into an absorptive sponge leading to a thickened wetland edge; and in New Aqueous City's infiltration basins on land and inflatable bathymetric airbags offshore, inverting the notion of a fortified edge.

With the exception of Oyster-tecture's oyster beds and Working Waterline's recycled-glass reef, the proposals focus on the waterfront edge, which is reworked, crenellated, and softened. Although no new inhabited islands or archipelagos in the bay have been proposed, all of the teams embrace the notion that it is necessary and appropriate to construct on and in the water. Perhaps this is the exhibition's most significant contribution to public discussion. It is evident in recent policy—including *Vision 2020: New York City Comprehensive Waterfront Plan,* recently issued by the New York City Department of City Planning—that building ecologies on and in the water is no longer anathema. In fact, there may even be a convergence of interests, as the Port Authority of New York and New Jersey considers the possibility of developing island wetlands as a strategy for both disposing of clean dredge spoils and enriching the bay ecology, and as the United States Environmental Protection Agency sponsors an oyster reef and wetland study project.

With impending sea level rise, the stakes have never been higher. The inspired collaborative solutions of these five teams—ranging, in terms of scale, from the cellular (oyster spats) to the sublime (an aggregate glass reef)—do much more than just protect our region from flooding. Their projects address energy production and use, ecological health, waste management, and global green shipping. Perhaps most importantly, they capture the imagination of a regional community, celebrating the body of water that Giovanni da Verrazano called "a very agreeable location situated within two prominent hills" upon his first sighting of the Upper Bay in 1524.[9]

CONTROLLED FLOODING AND THE MISSISSIPPI DELTA

Shortly after the *Rising Currents* exhibition opened in March 2010, we were invited by Jonathan Solomon to present our Palisade Bay project in the exhibition *Workshopping: An American Model of Architectural Practice,* which he was organizing with Michael Rooks of Atlanta's High Museum of Art for the United States Pavilion at the Venice Biennale's 12th International Architecture Exhibition. We decided to extend our research beyond the New York–New Jersey Upper Bay to the place that in many ways inspired us in the first place: New Orleans and the Mississippi River Delta. The loss of wetlands from subsidence in the delta is dramatic; many scientists agree that healthy wetlands help absorb the

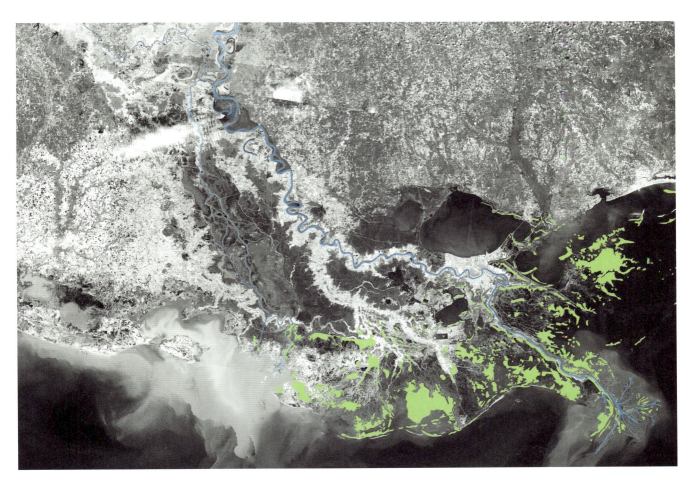

Mississippi River Delta wetland loss (in green) since 1900. The wetlands are disappearing at a rate of 25 square miles (about 64 km²) per year. Michael Blum and Harry Roberts, Coastal Sustainability Studio, Louisiana State University

force of storm surges. Sea level rise will certainly have its most devastating effects in areas where the land is also subsiding; the extremely flat terrain and soft sediment of the Mississippi River Delta is surely the foremost example of this condition. Here, one must address not only rising sea levels but also sinking ground, leading to a proposal for a parallel adaptive strategy of land building. Unlike the deep fjord geology of New York Harbor and the Hudson River estuary, carved by slow glacial movement, the terrain of the Mississippi River Delta is broad and expansive in its flatness, a landscape of slow-moving but dynamic mud. Working with the Louisiana State University Coastal Sustainability Studio, led by Jori Erdman, Jeffrey Carney, Lynne Carter, and Elizabeth Mossop, and oceanographers and coastal scientists Robert Twilley and Clint Willson, we held a charette in May and June 2010 to visualize the effects of Twilley's proposal for five great diversions of the Mississippi River's water and sediment.[10] These would rebuild the region's wetlands and alleviate subsidence to allow for what he calls "controlled flooding." With a group of Princeton University graduate students, we built two large models of the continuous bathymetry and topography of both the New York–New Jersey Upper Bay and the Mississippi River Delta, directly manifesting our idea of the continuity of land and water and presenting water as volumetric form. These scale models, which render the land in medium-density fiberboard and the water as a suspended acrylic volume above, were the focus of an installation that succinctly presented the position of our Palisade Bay project and Twilley's proposal for Mississippi River diversions.

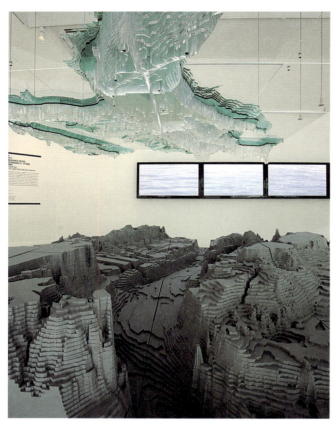

TOP LEFT AND RIGHT: New York–
New Jersey Upper Bay topographic/
bathymetric model in *Workshopping:
An American Model of Architectural
Practice*, United States Pavilion, 12th
International Architecture Exhibition,
Venice Biennale, 2010. Catherine
Seavitt Studio and Guy Nordenson
and Associates

BOTTOM LEFT AND RIGHT: Mississippi
River Delta topographic/bathymetric
model. The clear rods on the suspended
water volume indicate the depth of
the Mississippi River. In *Workshopping:
An American Model of Architectural
Practice.* Catherine Seavitt Studio and
Guy Nordenson and Associates

ABOVE: Harold N. Fisk. *Map of Ancient Courses of the Mississippi River Meander Belt (Cape Girardeau, MO–Donaldsonville, LA).* Plate 22, Sheet 13. 1944. US Army Corps of Engineers

BELOW: Transformation of the meandering Mississippi River system into a highly engineered and constructed landscape, in support of navigable waterways and a precise flood-control strategy. 1958. US Army Corps of Engineers

RIGHT: Aerial view of the Old River Control Structure (completed in 1963), at the divergence of the Atchafalaya and Mississippi rivers, 1999.

The Mississippi River once took a meandering course along an alluvial plain, changing its route slowly over thousands of years. Since the nineteenth century, it has become a constructed landscape supporting both flood protection and navigable waterways serving industry. In 1879 the engineer James Eads intervened at the mouth of the Mississippi with projecting jetties fabricated from reed mattresses. The result was a newly channelized river with a greater speed of flow at its mouth that carried sediment along at a greater velocity. This engineering produced the desired result: the reduction of sedimentation at the mouth of the river and the improvement of navigability. But scientists and engineers now recognize a negative consequence. Rather than being deposited to create wetlands, the rich sediment carried along the great watershed of the Mississippi was dumped off the edge of the continental shelf of the Gulf of Mexico.

The devastating flood of 1927 compelled Congress to enact the Flood Control Act of 1928, which eventually led to the construction of the Old River Control Structure, started in 1954 and completed in 1963. This structure maintains the Mississippi River's current path by diverting flow to the Atchafalaya River just north of the state line separating Mississippi and Louisiana. Thirty percent of the upstream Mississippi River flow is sent down the Atchafalaya at the Old River Control Structure and the remaining seventy percent down the Mississippi through New Orleans and into the Gulf of Mexico. Without this structure, the waters of the Mississippi would again shift slowly westward toward the course of the Atchafalaya.[11] The implementation of this and many other flood-control structures and levees along the river has reduced the deposition of sediment to the delta's wetlands and coastal basins. However, at the Wax Lake Delta Outlet, an artificial channel created by the US Army Corps of Engineers, the Atchafalaya has since 1973 been forming a new delta with depositional sediment—the only place in the region that is gaining ground.

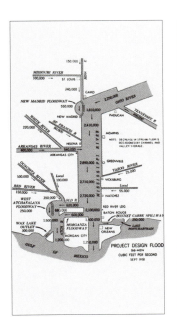

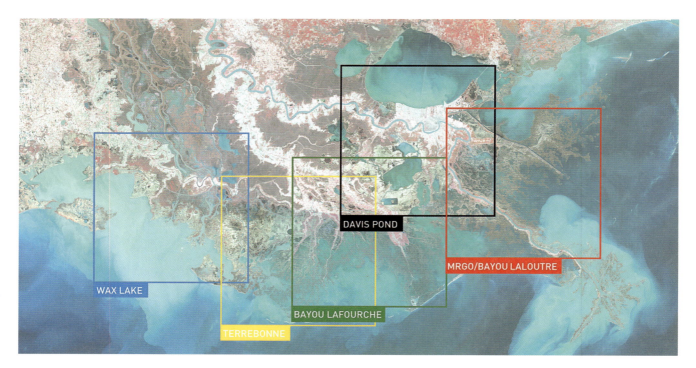

WAX LAKE

DAVIS POND

MRGO/BAYOU LALOUTRE

BAYOU LAFOURCHE

TERREBONNE

Hoping to emulate this land-building success, Twilley and Willson have proposed the construction of five new diversions of the Mississippi River, recreating a constructed landscape in which sediment will again be carried along with freshwater and deposited, thus forming new land. These locations, from west to east, include Wax Lake, Terrebonne, Bayou Lafourche, Davis Pond, and Mississippi River Gulf Outlet (MRGO)/ Bayou La Loutre. The strategy is to restore the river's role as a conduit for sediment, balancing man-made structures with natural coastal processes. The additional diversions would also promote flood control and navigation. For example, Bayou Lafourche, near the geographic center of the delta, was once a main distributary channel of the Mississippi River. In 1903 a dam was constructed across its head at Donaldsonville, and now it is a small stream that runs alongside Louisiana State Highway 1, linking a chain of towns. The proposed diversion would reopen the bayou, widening it to convey more water and sediment, and thus rebuild wetlands in Terrebonne and Barataria bays. This would represent a serious disruption of the existing social and rural conditions along the bayou and would likely be resisted by the communities. Yet perhaps an integrated design of soft infrastructure and ecologies that would both protect and improve the existing circumstances along Bayou Lafourche would ultimately find acceptance.

The project exhibited at the Venice Biennale also envisions a rearrangement of the flows of water and sediment on a scale not imagined since the 1963 completion of the Old River Control Structure. Our team worked with Willson to develop a series of controlled-flooding flow diagrams integrating the Atchafalaya/Mississippi River system with the five proposed diversions, creating various flow scenarios for the Mississippi. The diagrams illustrate the necessity of taking advantage of peak flows during spring flood events by opening the diversions to freshwater and sediment while controlling the volume of water channeled to each diversion as a flood-control measure. This could be the basis for a new strategy for soft infrastructure that is both protective and constructive. Over time, the process would reestablish vibrant wetlands in the delta region, create barriers against storm surges, and restore dynamic natural habitats.

Bayou Lafourche diversion site, once a main distributary channel of the Mississippi River. Guy Nordenson and Associates and the Louisiana State University Coastal Sustainability Studio

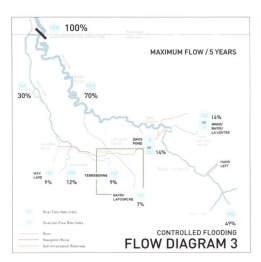

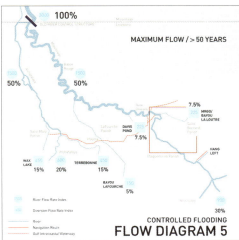

CLIMATE-CHANGE ADAPTATION DESIGN AND ENGINEERING

> I don't want to be a product of my environment, I want the environment
> to be a product of me.
> —Francis "Frank" Costello (Jack Nicholson) in *The Departed,* 2006

The Promethean truth of climate change is that it is the direct consequence of the very technical prowess we would depend on to arrest its course. And it is difficult to be optimistic when one reads daily of the skepticism, sometimes genuine, but mostly instrumental and self-interested, that confronts efforts at mitigating climate change by reducing carbon and other greenhouse gas emissions. It is tragic, all too human, and frightening at times—a dark narrative that could very well end badly.

Since we prepared our research for *On the Water: Palisade Bay,* the consensus of scientists monitoring the melting ice caps in Greenland and the Antarctic is that sea level will rise by at least 3 feet (0.9 m) by 2100.[12] At the beginning of the *Rising Currents* workshop, this figure seemed to be the upper limit, but now it may well be what we must expect. And of course sea level will continue to rise after 2100, as well. We are still unprepared either to arrest the accumulation of greenhouse gas or to confront the necessity of climate-change adaptation. In time there will be disasters, whether relentless changes in weather patterns, repeated flooding, or the sudden dissolution of major glaciers or ice caps, and the world will come to its senses as it once did to confront the destruction of the ozone layer by fluorocarbons.

If climate change is of our own doing, how would we best adapt to it? First it is necessary to change our own minds and the minds of others on the subject. While policy and politics can help, we believe that images, design, and art will lead the way. As the great metallurgist and historian of science Cyril Stanley Smith showed, it is art that leads the way to technology and inspires science. Humans used steel—if mostly to destructive ends—long before they knew what made it so strong and hard. The craftsmen of the Damascus blades and Japanese samurai swords had a sophisticated understanding of how to form and forge complex and balanced steel blades that also displayed their properties in gorgeous grain patterns. It was long after these craftsmen had perfected their art that scientists unraveled the atomic nature of steel alloys.

As John McPhee wrote in a 1987 article (and later in the book *The Control of Nature*),

> The Mississippi River, with its sand and silt, has created most of Louisiana,
> and it could not have done so by remaining in one channel. If it had, southern
> Louisiana would be a long narrow peninsula reaching into the Gulf of Mexico.
> Southern Louisiana exists in its present form because the Mississippi River
> has jumped here and there within an arc about two hundred miles wide,
> like a pianist playing with one hand—frequently and radically changing course,
> surging over the left or the right bank to go off in utterly new directions.[13]

We must align our infrastructure with the flows and courses of these and other waters, and, where necessary, make protective structures that share nature's adaptability. As we continue to imagine and represent the complex natures of resilient, soft infrastructure, then the engineering science, the designs, and the will necessary to bring them about may too emerge.

NOTES

1. "The god am I, whose yellow water flows/Around these fields, and fattens as it goes:/Tiber my name—among the rolling floods/Renowned on earth, esteemed among the gods./This is my certain seat. In times to come,/My waves shall wash the walls of mighty Rome!" Virgil, *The Aeneid*, book 8, trans. John Dryden (New York: Macmillan, 1965), 90.

2. Guy Nordenson, Catherine Seavitt, and Adam Yarinsky, *On the Water: Palisade Bay* (Berlin: Hatje Cantz/The Museum of Modern Art, 2010).

3. The 2007 Latrobe Prize was awarded to Guy Nordenson and Associates (GNA), Catherine Seavitt Studio (CSS), and Architecture Research Office (ARO). Guy Nordenson, PE SE, professor of architecture and structural engineering at Princeton University's School of Architecture and partner at GNA, was the overall project director. Nordenson worked with Professor James Smith of Princeton University's Department of Civil and Environmental Engineering and with Michael Tantala to direct the engineering analyses and infrastructural design. CSS principal Catherine Seavitt, AIA, and ARO principal Adam Yarinsky, FAIA, oversaw the urban planning, architecture, and landscape design. Seavitt also provided the ecological analyses. Additional key team members included ARO principal Stephen Cassell, AIA, and Lizzie Hodges and Marianne Koch of GNA.

4. Vivien Gornitz, Stephen Couch, and Ellen K. Hartig, "Impacts of Sea Level Rise in the New York City Metropolitan Area," *Global and Planetary Change* 32 (2002): 72.

5. Ibid., 85.

6. The Intergovernmental Panel on Climate Change concluded that it is "likely" that tropical cyclones will be more intense in the future. See R. K. Pachauri and A. Reisinger, eds., *Climate Change 2007: Synthesis Report: Contribution of Working Groups I, II and III to the Fourth Assessment Report of the Intergovernmental Panel on Climate Change* (Geneva: IPCC, 2007), 47.

7. Gornitz et al., "Impacts of Sea Level Rise," 66.

8. Malcolm J. Bowman et al., *Hydrologic Feasibility of Storm Surge Barriers to Protect the Metropolitan New York–New Jersey Region: Final Report to HydroQual, Inc.* (Stony Brook, N.Y.: Marine Sciences Research Center, State University of New York, March 2005).

9. This description is from a letter to King Francis I of France. See Lawrence C. Wroth, *The Voyages of Giovanni da Verrazzano, 1524–1528* (New Haven, Conn.: Yale University Press, 1970).

10. The Louisiana State University Coastal Sustainability Studio is committed to developing pragmatic, transdisciplinary, systems-oriented techniques for reducing environmental vulnerability and enhancing community resiliency along the dynamic coast of Louisiana. The team includes Jori Erdman, AIA, Jeffrey Carney, Lynne Carter, PhD, Elizabeth Mossop, Robert Twilley, PhD, and Clint Willson, PhD PE, with assistance from Natalie Yates and Ursula Emery McClure and Michael A. McClure of emerymcclure architecture.

11. "The Mississippi River and Tributaries Project," US Army Corps of Engineers: New Orleans District, May 19, 2004, http://www.mvn.usace.army.mil/pao/bro/misstrib.htm.

12. Justin Gillis, "As Glaciers Melt, Science Seeks Data on Rising Seas," *New York Times*, November 13, 2010, http://www.nytimes.com/2010/11/14/science/earth/14ice.html.

13. John McPhee, "Atchafalaya," *The New Yorker*, February 23, 1987, http://www.newyorker.com/archive/1987/02/23/1987_02_23_039_TNY_CARDS_000347146. *The Control of Nature* (New York: Farrar, Straus & Giroux, 1989), 5.

PROJECTS

FEBRUARY 17, 2010

The *Rising Currents* exhibition provides us with a
model of how the innovative use of both structural and
non-structural elements can help us withstand the
impacts of climate change while making the city more
sustainable. It also emphasizes the need to involve a
wide variety of disciplines, experts, and stakeholders
in developing resilience strategies to ensure that all
possibilities are explored. I left my tour of the P.S.1
studios not only impressed with the tremendous work
of the teams, but with a great deal of optimism about
our ability to meet the challenges before us.

—Adam Freed, Deputy Director, New York City Mayor's
Office of Long-Term Planning and Sustainability, on the
Rising Currents blog

FROM MoMA PS1 TO THE MUSEUM OF MODERN ART

	10.20.09	11.16.09	11.23.09	12.12.09
NEW URBAN GROUND				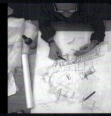
WORKING WATERLINE				
WATER PROVING GROUND				
OYSTER-TECTURE				
NEW AQUEOUS CITY				

ORIENTATION
The teams visit site locations in advance of the residency and workshop at MoMA PS1.

ARCHITECTS-IN-RESIDENCE
The teams begin work in their studios at MoMA PS1.

STUDIO VISIT
The teams present their work in progress to visitors including scientists from the Marine Sciences Research Center at the State University of New York at Stony Brook.

OPEN HOUSE
The studios are open to the public. Visitors meet the teams and view their work in progress.

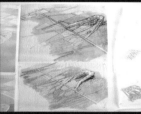   

STUDIO VISIT
The teams present their work in progress to visitors including officials from the Governors Island Preservation and Education Corporation, the Port Authority of New York and New Jersey, and the New York City Mayor's Office of Long-Term Planning and Sustainability.

OPEN HOUSE
The studios are open to the public. Visitors meet the teams and view the models, drawings, and renderings that will be included in the *Rising Currents* exhibition at MoMA. Team leaders present their final project proposals.

STUDIO VISIT
The teams present their project proposals to visitors including officials from the New York State Department of Environmental Conservation Office of Environmental Justice and members of the New York State Sea Level Rise Task Force Community Resilience and Adaptation Workshop.

STUDIO VISIT
The teams present their project proposals to members of the Hudson-Fulton-Champlain Quadricentennial Commission.

NEW URBAN GROUND

STEPHEN CASSELL AND ADAM YARINSKY, ARCHITECTURE RESEARCH OFFICE (ARO), AND SUSANNAH C. DRAKE, DLANDSTUDIO

New Urban Ground is a new paradigm for city infrastructure in Lower Manhattan, combining soft and hard solutions. Beginning in the 1600s, Dutch colonists in the region built docks to facilitate trade, fortifications to prevent attack, and seawalls to protect the growing city from its watery lifeline, gradually erasing Manhattan's marshy edges. Now the city's modern seawall faces storm surges it will not be able to withstand. In New Urban Ground, downtown is simultaneously protected and "greened" through the introduction of absorptive wetlands and parklands, a greater emphasis on public transit, and streets that have been reconceived as environmentally productive spaces.

The history of urban modernization can be traced through roadways, which perform key functions beyond surface transportation, providing important rights-of-way for freshwater and wastewater infrastructure. In earlier periods, planners imagined streets as constructed machines, working to contain and manage the forces of nature. In New Urban Ground, Lower Manhattan is paved with a mesh of cast concrete and plants selected for their tolerance to pollution and saltwater. These porous green streets act as a sponge for rainwater in a new organic system designed to respond resiliently to daily tidal flows and occasional storm surges. The new wetlands provide an additional buffer against tides and restore the natural dynamics of the island.

TEAM MEMBERS
Neil Patel and Michael Jejon Yeung, ARO; Lauren Barry, Yong K. Kim, and Leah Kiren Solk, dlandstudio; and Elliott Landry Smith

PROJECT SITE
Lower Manhattan

OPPOSITE: Lower Manhattan in 2100. In accordance with New Urban Ground, cuts into the island have created urban estuaries. Dark-green areas are upland parks, medium-green areas are freshwater wetlands, and light-green areas are saltwater marshes. The outer dotted line represents high tide based on a projected 6-foot (1.8 m) sea level rise. The inner dotted line represents the area that would be inundated by a 24-foot (7.3 m) storm surge from a Category 2 hurricane—approximately 61 percent of Lower Manhattan. The plan adds 2 miles (3.2 km) of shoreline to Manhattan, and a new, continuous ecosystem encompasses the island's edge.

Proposed "greening" of Lower Manhattan. Parks and wetlands create new ecosystems, facilitating the ecological interconnectivity of the region, improving water quality, and enhancing opportunities for habitat growth.

SITE PLAN EXTENTS

Urban estuaries supporting saltwater and freshwater wetlands alternate with areas zoned for development, creating a balance between ecological and economic sustainability. Streets within the storm-surge flood zone are engineered for three different water-carrying capacities: absorption (Level 1), distribution (Level 2), and retention (Level 3).

URBAN ESTUARY AT NORTH MOORE STREET
Here a saltwater marsh mitigates the force of incoming water in the event of a storm surge. North Moore is a Level 2 street, designed to carry runoff and storm-surge flooding off the land and out into the harbor.

URBAN ESTUARY AT LIBERTY STREET
The steep bathymetry of the harbor necessitates cuts into the urban landmass to create shallow water. Shallows support the plant and animal ecosystems that, in turn, ameliorate the impact of upland runoff. A series of elevated walkways creates a platform for recreation, allowing people to occupy the estuary without disrupting the natural habitat.

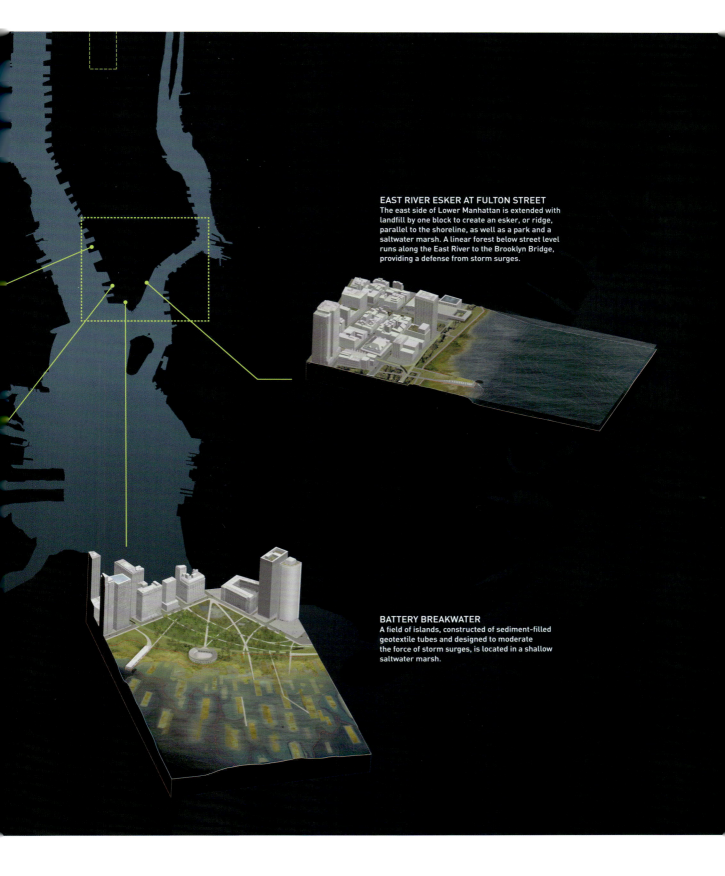

EAST RIVER ESKER AT FULTON STREET
The east side of Lower Manhattan is extended with landfill by one block to create an esker, or ridge, parallel to the shoreline, as well as a park and a saltwater marsh. A linear forest below street level runs along the East River to the Brooklyn Bridge, providing a defense from storm surges.

BATTERY BREAKWATER
A field of islands, constructed of sediment-filled geotextile tubes and designed to moderate the force of storm surges, is located in a shallow saltwater marsh.

URBAN ESTUARY AT LIBERTY STREET

FULTON STREET
Much of Lower Manhattan is transformed into a network of green spaces as automobiles give way to mass transit. This Level 2 street absorbs rainfall and distributes it to local plantings and wetlands.

TRANSVERSE
A series of pile-supported recreational walkways is connected to the city streets.

BOAT BASIN
Calm, deep water accommodates small boat traffic.

LIBERTY STREET

FERRY STOP
The steep bathymetry is maintained to provide draft for boats.

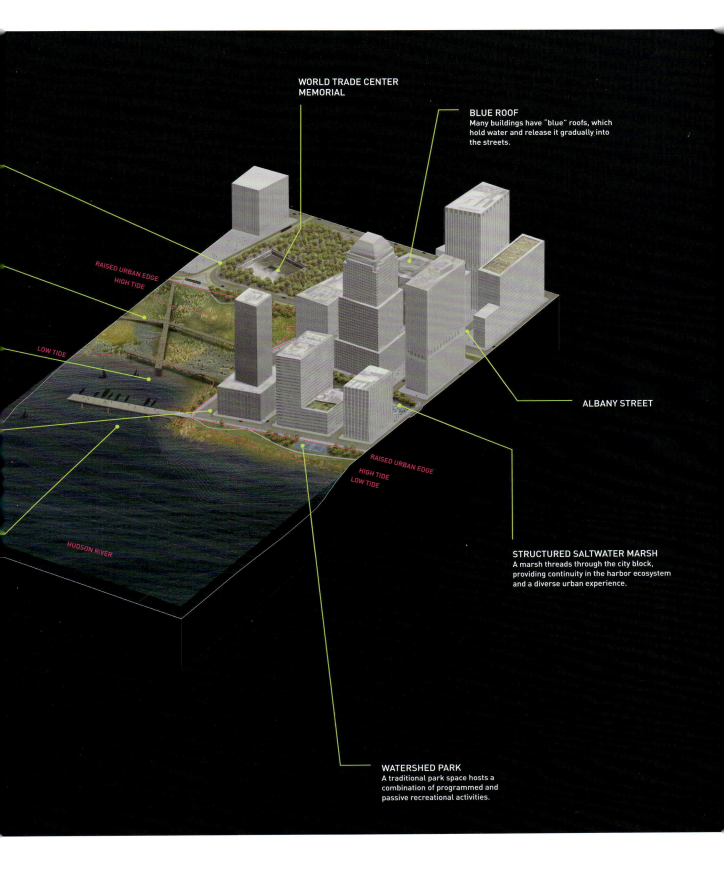

WORLD TRADE CENTER
MEMORIAL

BLUE ROOF
Many buildings have "blue" roofs, which
hold water and release it gradually into
the streets.

RAISED URBAN EDGE
HIGH TIDE

LOW TIDE

ALBANY STREET

RAISED URBAN EDGE
HIGH TIDE
LOW TIDE

HUDSON RIVER

STRUCTURED SALTWATER MARSH
A marsh threads through the city block,
providing continuity in the harbor ecosystem
and a diverse urban experience.

WATERSHED PARK
A traditional park space hosts a
combination of programmed and
passive recreational activities.

Western Parkway

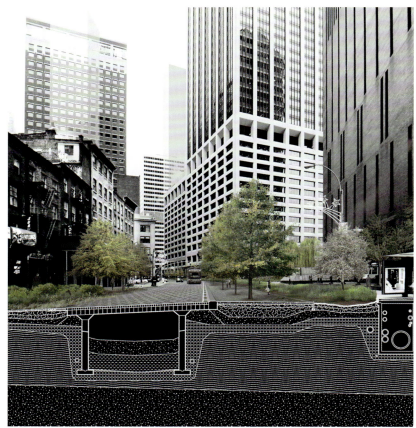

Water Street

WESTERN PARKWAY
West Street is reconstructed and renamed
Western Parkway. Much of its width is given
over to green space, a light-rail transit loop,
pedestrian walkways, and bike paths.

WATER STREET
Water Street, a Level 3 street, runs parallel to the shoreline. Level 3 streets are
designed to hold storm-surge volume and
drain back to the harbor. The plants in
these zones are selected for their capacity
to withstand higher levels of salinity due to
inundation from storm surges.

COENTIES SLIP
A linear forest below street level, modeled
on the sunken forests of Fire Island, off
Long Island, New York, provides a first line
of defense against a storm surge. The tree
canopy is aligned with parkland on top of
the East River Esker.

BROADWAY AND HANOVER SQUARE
Public and private utility infrastructure is
housed in accessible waterproof vaults
beneath the sidewalk. These vaults are
divided into two parts: private utilities (dry
systems, such as electricity and telecom-
munications) and public utilities (wet
systems such as water, gas, and sewers).

Coenties Slip

Broadway

Hanover Square

Q&A

WHAT ASPECTS OF *ON THE WATER* HELPED YOU FRAME YOUR PROJECT? DID YOU EVER DEPART FROM THE ANALYSIS OUTLINED IN *ON THE WATER*?

Stephen Cassell and Adam Yarinsky, Architecture Research Office (ARO), and Susannah C. Drake, dlandstudio

On the Water quantified what sea level rise will mean for the upper harbor of New York and New Jersey and offered strategies for how the city might transform its waterfront in response. However, New Urban Ground reaches beyond the waterfront. The green spaces on our drawings and model indicate a continuous eco-system extending from the interior of Manhattan to the water's edge. This ecological infrastructure, which consists of green streets and wetlands, absorbs and distributes storm water and was designed according to specific data on how water from a storm surge is best processed. New Urban Ground is more than a response to the need to control the input and outflow of water; it also provides an opportunity to transform the urban experience.

Q2

HOW DOES THIS PROJECT DIFFER FROM YOUR PRACTICE TO DATE?

The *Rising Currents* workshop was unique. While our studio space was located at ARO's offices, not MoMA PS1, we participated in the pinups, critiques, and public open houses. The comments we received from people who attended these events were invaluable. Encampment of the designers in one space for a period of intense creative development was also extraordinarily productive. It was great to work alongside our peers on the other teams and to receive comments and feedback from them. These exchanges were as good as the formal pinups. Critiques with Barry Bergdoll were also influential, as were opportunities to present the work to guests brought into the process by MoMA, including staff from New York City's Office of Emergency Management and Department of City Planning, the state Department of Environmental Conservation, and other agencies.

Q3

WHAT ASPECTS OF YOUR PROJECT WOULD YOU DEVELOP OR CHANGE?

We produced many more ideas than we could develop or display in the exhibition. How the city would change in response to different flooding scenarios is something we would have liked to show in greater detail. This includes what storm surges might look like and how wetland edge conditions will change over several decades. Visualizing how plants are affected by water flow from a surge would also have been useful, as such changes would affect the character of public space for some time after a surge. Although we deliberately focused on public space, we would also have liked to present how buildings might be modified or used differently in response to rising waters. Going forward, we would like to perform a cost-benefit analysis to make the case for proactive policy measures. We hope to work with civil and geotechnical engineers to develop the street section that we presented in the exhibit and test and push our ideas through further study and pilot projects.

Q4

WHAT ASPECTS OF YOUR PROJECT ARE SPECIFIC TO NEW YORK, AND WHAT WOULD BE VALUABLE FOR OTHER CITIES FACING SEA LEVEL RISE?

Ideas from New Urban Ground are applicable to every waterfront city with combined sewer overflow issues. The morphology would change with each local application, but the basic relationship between street section and water's edge would remain. These ideas could probably exist at the greatest intensity in New York. Other cities have the luxury of more open space. The cost-benefit analysis would change in each application, of course, but in some cities it might be cheaper to build these systems than in New York. Variations might also reflect different cultural uses of urban public space.

Q5

HOW WOULD YOU FORMULATE THE BRIEF IF YOU WERE DESIGNING A COMPETITION LIKE THIS ONE FOR ALL OF NEW YORK CITY, NOT JUST YOUR OWN ZONE?

The brief might ask designers to look at the city across different scales of time. One team would design the city for ten years out, another for twenty-five years, another for seventy-five years in the future. The brief might also organize designers' work by city agency, tasking them to create projects that can only be implemented by specific agencies or that demand work across city, state, and federal jurisdictions that control the water's edge.

Q6

WHAT DO YOU THINK THE FUTURE HOLDS FOR ARCHITECTS WORKING ON SEA LEVEL RISE AND CLIMATE CHANGE AND FOR PUBLIC OFFICIALS, BUILDING DEVELOPERS, AND CITIZENS?

New science is needed to define the effects of wave action on the urban environment. This will create criteria needed to implement new designs. For example, what is the optimal shape and orientation for an artificial island? For a precedent, look at the seismic studies used to design buildings. Fifty years ago these didn't exist; today we take for granted that buildings can be designed to resist earthquakes. But this parallel has some limits: in the case of a changing climate, there also needs to be some discussion about where and what we build.

Dynamic modeling tools, such as geographic information systems (GIS) and parametric software, will be essential to understanding the built and natural world. These will allow us to understand the city's performance during severe weather conditions, whether that means heavy rain, storm surges, or sea level rise in general. We will all have to accommodate new, nonlinear systems of demarcation.

Today the public has only a limited understanding of sustainability, let alone how climate change will impact the built environment. It will be necessary for architects, developers, and public officials to create projects with manifold benefits for our quality of life that are readily understood. We're at a very early stage of development with sustainability, comparable to where personal computers might have been a few decades ago. Now it's urgent that we arrive as quickly as possible at the "iPhone" stage of sustainability—in which it is ubiquitous, popular, and effective.

OPPOSITE: Model of Lower Manhattan and New Urban Ground site plan extents and diagrams in the gallery.

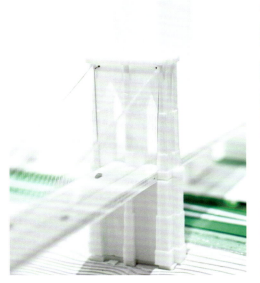

WORKING WATERLINE

MATTHEW BAIRD, MATTHEW BAIRD ARCHITECTS

Matthew Baird and his team tackled a site with features ranging from the low-lying lands of Bayonne, New Jersey—occupied primarily by an oil-tank farm and a military pier—to the residential areas of Staten Island along Kill Van Kull, largely on higher ground. The team imagined new natural and economic ecologies for the region, selecting among existing and potential landscape features and uses. In Working Waterline, World War II–era piers and warehouses have been transformed into a recycling facility, and disused oil tanks are used to create biofuel, fed by wastewater. The new recycling facility turns the region's vast supply of discarded glass into the components of reefs, examples of which are dumped onto the local riverbed; the reef is a breakwater and, over time, it creates habitats for marsh grasses and other marine life that further attenuate storm surges. The proposal features a vast, sinuous berm (protecting contaminated areas from flooding) and an elevated, energy-generating "solar" path through the site for pedestrians and vehicles. Energy production and industry coexist with recreational opportunities—from kayaking among industrial artifacts of the twentieth century to swimming over the glass reefs. Working Waterline is an elevated, productive coast, rescued from ecological disaster—a regional economy stimulated by rising sea level, generating value from detritus.

TEAM MEMBERS
Kira Appelhans, Kristen Becker, Daniel Greenfield, Nim Lee, Ajay Manthripragada, Maria Milans del Bosch, and Juanita Wichienkuer

PROJECT SITE
Kill Van Kull and Bayonne, New Jersey

OPPOSITE: Working Waterline incorporates three interconnected categories of action: keep, add, and reuse. Red lines ("add") indicate pedestrian and bicycle paths. Areas marked in green ("keep") include existing salt marshes, utility buildings, and parkland. In blue ("reuse") are shipping piers, warehouses, and discarded glass in landfills.

Recycled-glass structures create a reef on the riverbed, attenuating the flow of water and creating a habitat for plant and animal life.

Biofuel plant

Glass reef

Kill Van Kull

Staten Island

KEEP: SOIL

More than a century of oil refining in Bayonne has contaminated the soil with petroleum and heavy metals—pollution that would spread if the land flooded. In Working Waterline, the area is protected from the incursion of water through the use of existing soil, a low-energy solution.

Contaminated soil that would be inundated in a 100-year flood is relocated, while soil that would be covered by a 500-year flood is contained with a bentonite (absorptive clay) cap and a protective berm made of soil dredged from Kill Van Kull.

Existing site with the proposed addition of a berm park and repurposed oil refineries for algal-oil biofuel.

REUSE: BIOFUEL

An algal-oil biofuel farm is established, a cost-effective alternative to the traditional petroleum refining it replaces on the site.

New York City's combined sewer (rainwater runoff, domestic sewage, and industrial wastewater) overflow (CSO) is diverted from the water-ways for use as fertilizer.

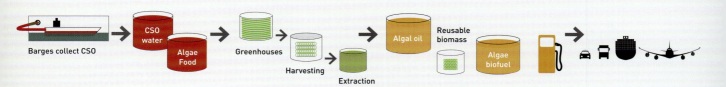

Barges collect CSO   CSO water   Algae Food   Greenhouses   Harvesting   Extraction   Algal oil   Reusable biomass   Algae biofuel

Algal-oil biofuel plant uses 27 billion gallons (102 billion l) of CSO per year, New York City's annual production.

2010
Injected bentonite wall, in red. Soil on the water side is relocated behind the wall. Soil behind the wall is capped and contained.

2020
A berm protects capped and contained contaminated soil from storm surges.

2070
Projected berm growth.

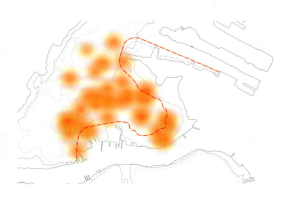

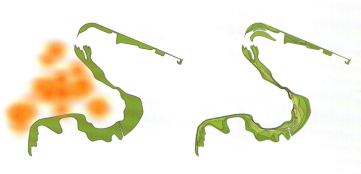

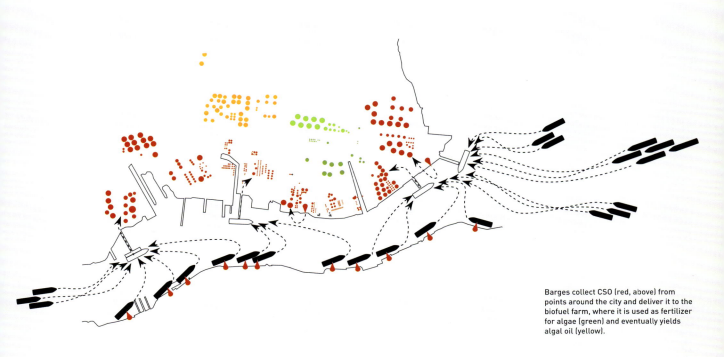

Barges collect CSO (red, above) from points around the city and deliver it to the biofuel farm, where it is used as fertilizer for algae (green) and eventually yields algal oil (yellow).

REUSE: SHIPPING PIER

The melting of the northern polar ice cap has affected shipping, shortening the passage from Japan to New York City by a week. The first commercial transportation of goods by water through the previously inaccessible Northeast Passage was made in 2009. In Working Waterline, the Bayonne shipping pier is revitalized as an active regional port, capitalizing on this route change.

Existing site with repurposed oil refineries for algal-oil biofuel and the proposed additions of a berm park, shipping piers, glass-recycling facilities, and glass reefs.

REUSE: GLASS

Glass in existing landfill is repurposed into modular reef-building units that resemble toy jacks. They are produced in a new glass-recycling plant, employing an inexpensive, locally sourced, and readily available material in a new regional industry. The wave-attenuating reefs are heavy enough to withstand water currents and are textured to support the development of animal and plant life.

43,000 tons recycled
50,000 tons in landfill

1   10   20   30   40   50

= 1,000 tons glass/year

EXISTING EXPORTS OF GLASS WASTE

To Asia

EXISTING SHIPPING: 27 days
Fukuoka, Japan, to New York via Panama Canal

FUTURE SHIPPING: 19 days
Fukuoka, Japan, to New York via Northeast Passage

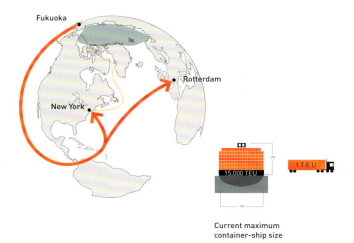

Fukuoka

New York

Rotterdam

15,000 TEU

1 T.E.U

Current maximum
container-ship size

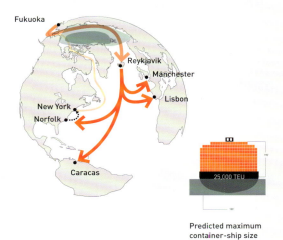

Fukuoka

Reykjavik

Manchester

New York

Lisbon

Norfolk

Caracas

25,000 TEU

Predicted maximum
container-ship size

Bayonne

100 TEU

PROPOSED REGIONAL IMPORTS OF GLASS WASTE

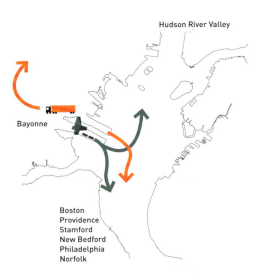

Hudson River Valley

Bayonne

Boston
Providence
Stamford
New Bedford
Philadelphia
Norfolk

REVITALIZED SHIPPING INDUSTRY EXPORTING GLASS JACKS

OPPOSITE: Working Waterline presentation in the gallery, with models of glass reef components. *Site Visit* (2010), industrial and natural artifacts gathered from the site and presented by artist Mark Dion, is in the foreground.

ABOVE: Glass reef component prototype with textured surface that will support marine life.

TOP: Detail aerial view of the section model, showing the berm park below a housing block at the end of a pier (top left) and the solar highway (top).

BOTTOM: Detail aerial view of the section model, showing a midpier area with solar highway passing above the glass-recycling facility and a glass-jack testing pool (far right).

Q&A

WHAT ASPECTS OF *ON THE WATER* HELPED YOU FRAME YOUR PROJECT? DID YOU EVER DEPART FROM THE ANALYSIS OUTLINED IN *ON THE WATER*?

Matthew Baird, Matthew Baird Architects

On the Water was an astounding body of research. Two ideas in particular were relevant to Working Waterline. First was the concept of repurposing industrial waste to create new habitats for marine life, which is part of a broader conversation about ecology and sustainability within old, messy urban landscapes like New York City and Bayonne, New Jersey. Second was the idea of reexamining parts of the urban fabric that we take for granted and looking deeper into how systems work within this fabric. Our project went a little further with these ideas; we looked at global systems—in particular global economic and natural systems—within the Kill Van Kull site. The realization that rising sea level would engender a new wave of industrial development due to evolving shipping routes led to our own research on shipping, global trade routes, and economic patterns.

Q2

HOW DOES THIS PROJECT DIFFER FROM YOUR PRACTICE TO DATE?

It is typical in our studio to assemble an interdisciplinary team to tackle the particularities of each new project. For *Rising Currents* we were able to include contemporary artists, shipping consultants, and ecologists at the earliest stage of design. These consultants led us to new territories, introducing ideas that were tested through the design process. Of course we would love to work with a multifaceted team for all our projects, but it was definitely due to MoMA that this became possible. Contemporary artists like Mark Dion and Matthew Ritchie, whom we worked with from the inception of our study, took us out of our architectural milieu.

I feel similarly enthusiastic about the open houses. Since my firm has so far been engaged with private works, it is often not

until after a project is published that people outside the office can experience and talk about the work. Our final project really was a response to all the input we received during the many months of work, critique, and dialogue.

Q3

WHAT ASPECTS OF YOUR PROJECT WOULD YOU DEVELOP OR CHANGE?

By the end of the eight-week design process on this massive site we had just gotten to a point in our planning where we began contemplating architecture at a tectonic scale. For example, one of our section models in the exhibition slices through a housing block. We began to imagine new construction being connected through an iconic structural unit and by a new datum of landscapes and infra-structures, all elevated above the new floodplain. We were not able to fully develop the housing typology, but it is something that I would be eager to explore and refine in future projects. Creating new, unexpected programmatic combinations within a vibrant working waterline is a compelling direction for urban waterfronts in flux.

Q4

WHAT ASPECTS OF YOUR PROJECT ARE SPECIFIC TO NEW YORK, AND WHAT WOULD BE VALUABLE FOR OTHER CITIES FACING SEA LEVEL RISE?

Our idea of "curating the edge" meant that we looked at the site to determine what could be recast as sites of production or leisure, and what elements, given their state of decay, could become reference points from which to measure a changing water level. For example, we repurposed existing oil refin-eries; the warehouses became sites for reef building, and a former gypsum plant became a destination for kayakers.

A second strategy, finding iconicity in the harbor, was an attempt to enhance the harbor's profile and address a host of problems posed by the rising sea level. To reframe the public attitude about waterfronts requires icons in the harbor. A series of glass reefs glistening in the Hudson could be a new

ecological infrastructure as compelling and necessary as, say, an iconic structure like the Brooklyn Bridge. While these strategies are site specific in our research, we believe these approaches could yield discoveries in a global context.

Q5

HOW WOULD YOU FORMULATE THE BRIEF IF YOU WERE DESIGNING A COMPETITION LIKE THIS ONE FOR ALL OF NEW YORK CITY, NOT JUST YOUR OWN ZONE?

When we began the design process we asked ourselves a series of questions that allowed us to focus on one particular location while also relating the site to its surroundings. I think these questions would be relevant to a competition for New York City:

1. How could we adapt and remake the water's edge in a way that would not further exacerbate climate change and sea level rise? What readily available materials might we use to do so?

2. How could we change public opinion about a tarnished landscape so as to highlight the beauty of a postindustrial seascape?

3. How could we reuse the latent energy stored in existing, soon-to-be obsolete infra-structure?

4. What is the future of shipping in New York's harbor?

5. How could we create a more vibrant working waterline?

Q6

WHAT DO YOU THINK THE FUTURE HOLDS FOR ARCHITECTS WORKING ON SEA LEVEL RISE AND CLIMATE CHANGE AND FOR PUBLIC OFFICIALS, BUILDING DEVELOPERS, AND CITIZENS?

Architects need to bring these issues to the forefront of their studies to make a real change. Initiatives like *Rising Currents* mark a shift in design culture as we gravitate to naturally efficient works and move away from pure aesthetic delights.

Since the exhibition we have been encouraged by ongoing discussions with city agencies as well as developers who came to us after visiting MoMA. A problem of this magnitude cannot be solved with public monies alone. There is an urgent need to create economic incentives and zoning initiatives to enlist the develop-ment industry in solutions to the issue of a rising sea.

OPPOSITE: Renderings, artwork, and models of Working Waterline in the gallery.

WATER PROVING GROUND

PAUL LEWIS, MARC TSURUMAKI, AND DAVID J. LEWIS, LTL ARCHITECTS

The team led by Paul Lewis, Marc Tsurumaki, and David J. Lewis of LTL Architects has envisioned a future for a zone including Liberty State Park, the Statue of Liberty, Ellis Island, and a section of New Jersey coastline (including Jersey City), an area created from landfill between 1860 and 1928 and that will, if left alone, all but disappear as sea level rises. The focus of the proposal is the protection and exploitation of lands that are subject to the continual dynamics of water.

Eschewing traditional defensive approaches, such as high seawalls, that sharpen and define the water's edge in order to protect it, the coastline in Water Proving Ground accommodates ambiguity between land and sea. The team proposes to increase the length of the shore by a factor of ten, to 45 miles (72.4 km), creating a wholly new landscape with an underlying structure of four raised "fingers" made by sculpting the existing landfill into a number of discrete "petri dish" areas. The new landscape is connected to the New Jersey mainland through a system of land and water transportation, so the park and productive areas are a true part of the region (unlike the current Liberty State Park, which is cut off by highway barriers). The team proposes a variety of uses for this hybrid land- and seascape—including agriculture, aquaculture, recreation, commerce, tourism, and ecological research—thus recapturing the historic role of the area as a vital point of exchange at the heart of New York Harbor.

TEAM MEMBERS
Aaron Forrest; Megan Griscom, OPEN Landscape Architecture; Perla Dís Kristirsdóttir, LTL Architects; and Yasmin Vobis

PROJECT SITE
Liberty State Park

OPPOSITE: Petri dishes are isolated environments for culturing cells, facilitating tests and studies. Water Proving Ground adopts the logic of the petri dish in its four built piers, incorporating a variety of discrete landscapes and habitats that juxtapose the natural and the artificial, production and recreation, land and water. These wedge-shaped zones comprise distinct areas and a variety of degrees of containment, from the highly compartmentalized (bioremediation areas) to very permeable (aquaculture zones). Within each wedge, the terrain slopes (see left), harnessing the dynamics of water flow and tidal change.

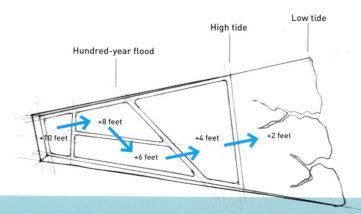

Low tide

High tide

Hundred-year flood

+10 feet

+8 feet

+6 feet

+4 feet

+2 feet

Wetlands

Runoff basin

Recreational fields

Docks

Liberty Science Center

Regional produce market

Invasive Species
Botanical Preserve

Tidal playground

Agriculture

CRRNJ terminal

Wastewater

Agriculture

Recreation

Community gardens

Bird habitat

Aquaculture

Turnpike operations

Water recreation

Water Lodge

Agriculture

Saltworks

Ellis Island

Bioremediation

Playing fields

Kelp forest

Wetland

Tidal park

Amphitheater

Hydrological testing

Fish hatchery

Liberty Island

Aquaculture Research and
Development Center

WATER PROVING GROUND

The proposal involves tactical adjustments to the topography of the site to exploit rising sea level and dynamic fluctuations in water level. These diagrams detail the phased development of the project and describe the different zones planned for each new pier.

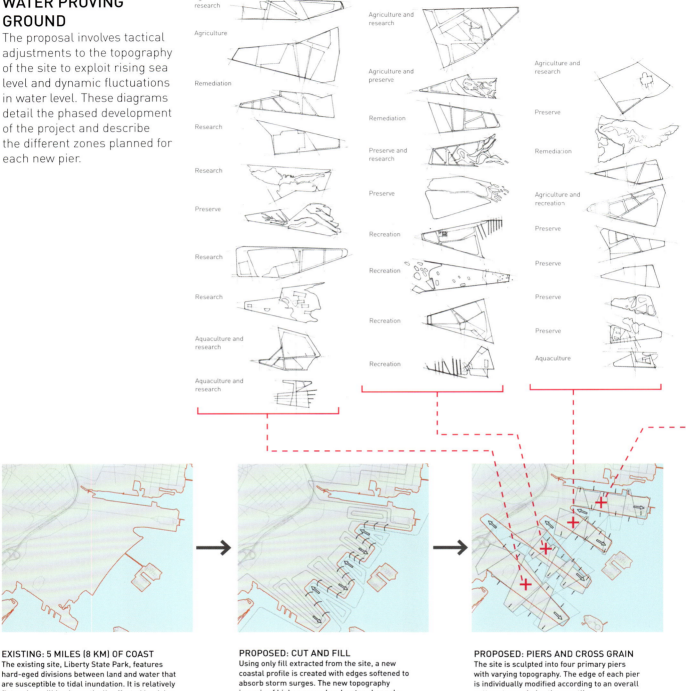

Agriculture and research

Agriculture

Remediation

Research

Research

Preserve

Research

Research

Aquaculture and research

Aquaculture and research

Agriculture and research

Agriculture and preserve

Remediation

Preserve and research

Preserve

Recreation

Recreation

Recreation

Recreation

Agriculture and research

Preserve

Remediation

Agriculture and recreation

Preserve

Preserve

Preserve

Preserve

Aquaculture

EXISTING: 5 MILES (8 KM) OF COAST
The existing site, Liberty State Park, features hard-eged divisions between land and water that are susceptible to tidal inundation. It is relatively flat and so will be dramatically affected by rising sea level.

PROPOSED: CUT AND FILL
Using only fill extracted from the site, a new coastal profile is created with edges softened to absorb storm surges. The new topography is a mix of higher ground and water channels.

PROPOSED: PIERS AND CROSS GRAIN
The site is sculpted into four primary piers with varying topography. The edge of each pier is individually modified according to an overall pattern to maximize the coastline.

2080 LOW TIDE

2010 LOW TIDE

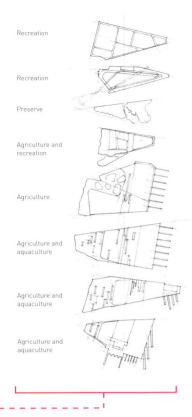

Recreation

Recreation

Preserve

Agriculture and recreation

Agriculture

Agriculture and aquaculture

Agriculture and aquaculture

Agriculture and aquaculture

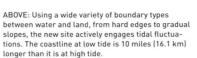

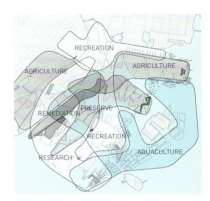

ABOVE: Using a wide variety of boundary types between water and land, from hard edges to gradual slopes, the new site actively engages tidal fluctuations. The coastline at low tide is 10 miles (16.1 km) longer than it is at high tide.

TOP RIGHT: Enhanced circulation routes engage the site, joining it to neighboring areas and bringing together land- and water-based transportation. New programmatic anchors on each of the piers activate the area, complementing the attractions of nearby Ellis Island and Liberty Island and incorporating the former Central Railroad of New Jersey terminal.

RIGHT: Tied into cycles of agriculture, aquaculture, recreation, and tourism, the redesigned site recaptures the historic role of the area as a vital point of exchange at the heart of New York Harbor.

BELOW: Water Proving Ground model on display in the gallery. The projection over the model shows the effects of the proposed piers on the site during low and high tides.

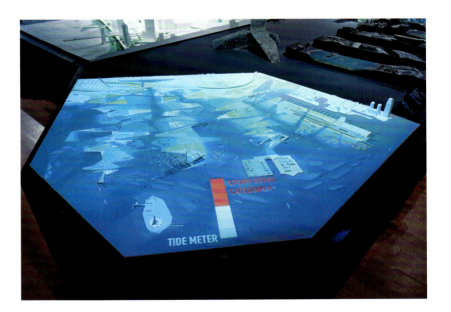

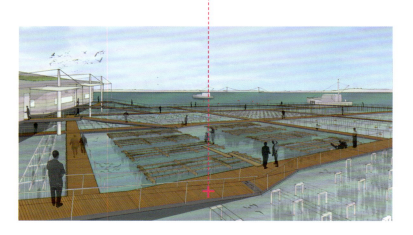

THE AQUACULTURE RESEARCH AND DEVELOPMENT CENTER (ARDC)

The center consists of a series of laboratories and testing beds. The second floor and roof are stable, but the floating docks rise and fall with the tide, allowing for controlled testing of aquatic species in the estuarine environment of the harbor. Studies at the ARDC focus on the interdependencies of farmed species, with the goal of developing a balanced and environmentally beneficial cultivation of the harbor.

2010 HIGH TIDE

2080 LOW TIDE

2010 LOW TIDE

AMPHITHEATER

An amphitheater adjacent to Liberty Island is a venue for large-scale outdoor concerts engaging the harbor (a long-time feature of the site). Camping barges and a marina allow for concert viewing from the water, while open-air seating and sloped lawns provide landside audiences with a backdrop of the Statue of Liberty. The floating stage can be repositioned to generate multiple relationships between performers and audiences; a secondary, enclosed space below the amphitheater is a controlled venue for smaller performances. Further up the pier is a tidal park—a watery, shifting field for recreational use, incorporating islands, pools, and beaches that emerge and disappear with tidal fluctuation.

HUNDRED-YEAR FLOOD

WATER LODGE

The Water Lodge provides for inhabitation of the site and is a base for the exploration of its various landscapes. Rising out of the watery landscape near Ellis Island on a forest of columns, the building shelters a marina for kayaks, a series of flooding terraces, and recreational pools integrated into the terrain. Boardwalks, docks, and boat trails link the lodge with campsites and diverse habitats, including the Invasive Species Botanical Preserve, which maintains the non-native plant species that are a legacy of the site's industrial past.

2010 HIGH TIDE

2010 LOW TIDE

2080 HIGH TIDE

2080 LOW TIDE

REGIONAL PRODUCE MARKET

A regional produce market revitalizes and extends the former
train shed and the historic Central Railroad of New Jersey
terminal, creating a locus of regional shopping and transportation.
It is a retail venue for local farmers and for the produce of the
experimental agricultural fields that make up the most northern
of the four piers. The building integrates ferry service with the
Hudson-Bergen Light Rail Line and car traffic, providing the major
point of transfer for goods and people into and out of the site.
The roof of the train shed blends visually with the adjacent agrar-
ian areas on a site that interweaves agriculture, aquaculture,
research, production, and commerce.

HUNDRED-YEAR FLOOD

Q1

WHAT ASPECTS OF *ON THE WATER* HELPED YOU FRAME YOUR PROJECT? DID YOU EVER DEPART FROM THE ANALYSIS OUTLINED IN *ON THE WATER*?

Paul Lewis, Marc Tsurumaki, and David J. Lewis, LTL Architects

On the Water's recasting of the harbor as a space that could foster new habitats and uses was fundamental to our proposal, Water Proving Ground. The valuation of water as a catalyst for urban transformation was the single most critical component of the study for our project, and it underwrote the diversity of uses that we imagined for our site. However, while the original study consigned the site to inundation, our strategy was to see this 1,200-acre landscape (around 5 km²) as a public resource for both New Jersey and New York City by maximizing its potential as a recreational amenity, a habitat with multiple ecologies, and a testing ground for new interfaces between the city and the harbor.

Other critical components of the study for us were the recognition of the complex and fluid nature of the boundary between land and water and the intentional exploitation of the elusive and changeable condition of the edge as an architectural strategy and a means of addressing sea level rise. However, whereas *On the Water* criticized "hard" engineering solutions and privileged more ecologically responsive "soft" infrastructure, our project engaged a range of edge conditions that varied from soft, sloping landscapes, subject to shift and fluctuation, to harder-edged, more compartmentalized zones for remediation and containment of toxic soils. Implicit in this is a recognition that multiple systems—both existing and emergent—will likely need to coexist.

Q2

HOW DOES THIS PROJECT DIFFER FROM YOUR PRACTICE TO DATE?

The vastness of our particular site meant that we had to reconsider radically the scale we were accustomed to working with as architects. We had to develop new tools and representational techniques for understanding the extensive territory and conveying the effects we were interested in generating, where small variations in section would have dramatic consequences in plan. Similarly, the project necessitated a different conception of time, taking into account the effects of sea level rise over decades and recognizing the daily cycles of the tides. This meant accepting and willfully engaging the uncertainties and lack of control implied by longer time frames and the effects of erosion, deposition, entropy, and growth.

The workshop was invaluable in generating insights and providing tools to contend with these more elusive aspects of the project. The landscape architects on our team and the diverse group of hydrologists, engineers, and ecologists that participated in the various sessions expanded our perspective on the vast range of issues impacting large-scale urban landscapes.

Q3

WHAT ASPECTS OF YOUR PROJECT WOULD YOU DEVELOP OR CHANGE?

The final project is a mosaic of diverse environments and uses based on active engagement with water. It would be fantastic to develop these typologies in detail, from tidal flats to artificial islands, exploring their effects and interactions.

Moreover, it would be fascinating to develop the various building components that inhabit this new amphibious ground. Building in this dynamic landscape would require new configurations predicated on the function of water as a performative element rather than simply a picturesque feature. Analogous to the often bizarre adaptations of biological organisms to extreme environmental conditions, inhabi-

tation of this unstable terrain would require invention, agility, and a radical rethinking of commonplace notions of stability, permanence, structure, ground, and enclosure.

Q4

WHAT ASPECTS OF YOUR PROJECT ARE SPECIFIC TO NEW YORK, AND WHAT WOULD BE VALUABLE FOR OTHER CITIES FACING SEA LEVEL RISE?

The project addresses New York Harbor but also acts as an experimental landscape for new techniques that could be applicable to other waterfront cities, such as diversifying uses. Whereas postindustrial sites are commonly repurposed as spaces of leisure and recreation—leading to a kind of monoculture—our project recuperates the industrial history of the site while combining it with new forms of access.

In addition, our site is typical of a fairly common condition in developed maritime zones: a postindustrial brownfield composed principally of landfill. These artificially constructed grounds aggregate around active harbors and often fringe major waterfront cities. Strategically reappropriating these areas as possible buffers to sea level rise and as active urban landscapes could lead to both mitigation and intensified use.

Q5

HOW WOULD YOU FORMULATE THE BRIEF IF YOU WERE DESIGNING A COMPETITION LIKE THIS ONE FOR ALL OF NEW YORK CITY, NOT JUST YOUR OWN ZONE?

We would resist the idea that it should be addressed by a single, monolithic plan. The terms of such a competition should generate flexible and adaptable frameworks that address the diversity of conditions—urban, social, and environmental—that characterize the water's edge. Avoiding a master-planning logic in favor of a more tactical and agile approach, the brief should to be constructed to skirt singular visions and encourage systemic approaches or repertoires of techniques that could be deployed in diverse ways.

Q6

WHAT DO YOU THINK THE FUTURE HOLDS FOR ARCHITECTS WORKING ON SEA LEVEL RISE AND CLIMATE CHANGE AND FOR PUBLIC OFFICIALS, BUILDING DEVELOPERS, AND CITIZENS?

Increasingly, the question will not simply be how to forestall or mitigate the effects of climate change but rather how to rethink received ideas about cities. Architects will have to conceive of their work less in terms of autonomous entities (however "green" the individual buildings may be) and instead as a part of more extensive systems, both natural and man-made. Architects will need to engage not only the infrastructural conditions that define our cities and landscapes but also recognize the imbrications of these networks with larger ecological, economic, and social fields.

Part of the challenge will be to open new, imaginative territory for architecture. Rather than instrumentalizing architecture as a solution to a problem, the desire should be to speculate about what a building, a landscape, or a city might be.

OPPOSITE: Models, renderings, and stills from the Water Proving Ground projection model in the gallery.

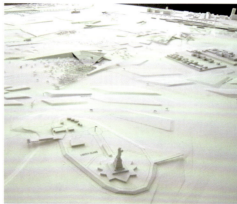

OYSTER-TECTURE

KATE ORFF, SCAPE

This team took on one of the most controversial zones, encompassing the highly polluted Gowanus Canal (designated a United States Environmental Protection Agency Superfund Site in 2010), Governors Island (currently being redeveloped into a major new park), the Red Hook area of Brooklyn, and the waters in between.

Engaging issues of water quality, encroaching tides, and community-based development, the team proposes to nurture the already active revitalization of a long-lost natural oyster reef in a phased process, developing an armature in the shallow waters of the Bay Ridge Flats, in Buttermilk Channel just south of Red Hook. The structure—a field of piles and a web of rope—is seeded with young oysters nurtured in a cleaned and revitalized Gowanus Canal. They begin their natural work of reef creation, stimulating the growth of other marine life (such as mussels and eelgrass), and clean millions of gallons of harbor water. A wave-attenuating structure, the reef protects the adjacent shoreline, on which there is a new, cleaner, water-based community with gardens fertilized with combined sewer overflow and reef-net and oyster development industries, where residents savor homegrown shellfish.

TEAM MEMBERS
Ben Abelman, Angela Chen-Mai Soong, Alice Feng, Steven Garcia, and Geneva Wirth, SCAPE

PROJECT SITE
Gowanus Canal, Red Hook, Governors Island, and Buttermilk Channel

OPPOSITE: Oyster-tecture implemented in the Bay Ridge Flats area, with reef, floating paths, anchorage areas for oyster harvesting, and constructed islands.

LEFT: The life cycle of the oysters begins in the Gowanus Canal, once home to New York's largest shellfish, where larvae are raised in floating upwelling system (FLUPSY) nursery rafts along the canal's edges. Spats are paraded to the Bay Ridge Flats and seeded on an armature, where they mature and aggregate over time.

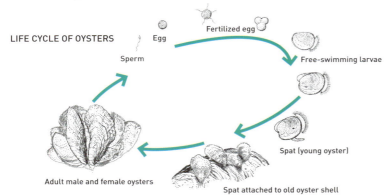

LIFE CYCLE OF OYSTERS

Egg

Sperm

Fertilized egg

Free-swimming larvae

Spat (young oyster)

Adult male and female oysters

Spat attached to old oyster shell

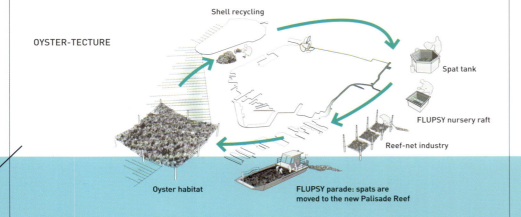

OYSTER-TECTURE

Shell recycling

Spat tank

FLUPSY nursery raft

Reef-net industry

Oyster habitat

FLUPSY parade: spats are moved to the new Palisade Reef

OYSTER-TECTURE

The development of "reef culture" reorients public life around the water. The Oyster-tecture life cycle, beginning in the Gowanus Canal, involves a series of components that not only fosters the growth of oysters but also provides recreational outlets for city dwellers and boosts the local economy—including a complex system of oyster husbandry, new pathways and parkland in the area, and a system of gardens that filter sewer overflow.

Water taxi plaza

Oyster harvesting

Oyster stick culture

Sand cap

Red Hook

Stabilized contaminants

Oyster bags

Historic bulkhead

Historic landfill

Rubble

Historic wetland

1. STICK CULTURE OYSTER FARMING   2. FLOATING UPWELLING SYSTEM [FLUPSY]   3. PUMICE FORMS

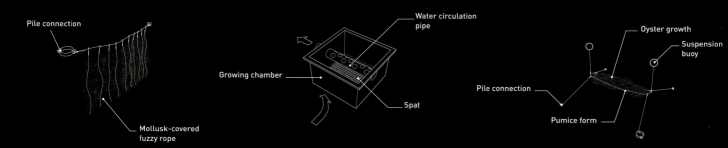

Pile connection

Mollusk-covered fuzzy rope

Water circulation pipe

Growing chamber

Spat

Oyster growth

Suspension buoy

Pile connection

Pumice form

FLUPSY path

Floodable soft edge

Oyster boat

Phytoremediation poplar trees

New York Canal School

Stormwater retention pools

Combined sewer
overflow treatment pond

Rain collection barrel

Combined sewer overflow pipe

Seaweed

5

6 Dam

4

Eelgrass habitat

Stabilized contaminants

Gowanus Canal

4. OYSTER NET

5. COMBINED SEWER OVERFLOW GARDEN

6. COMBINED SEWER OVERFLOW

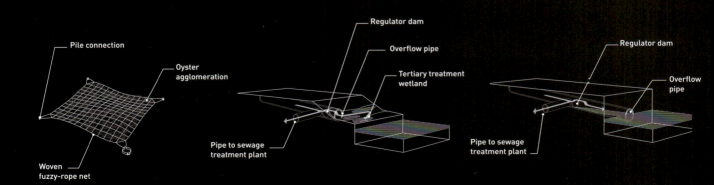

Pile connection

Oyster
agglomeration

Woven
fuzzy-rope net

Regulator dam

Overflow pipe

Tertiary treatment
wetland

Pipe to sewage
treatment plant

Regulator dam

Overflow
pipe

Pipe to sewage
treatment plant

BACK TO THE FUTURE

Oyster-tecture incorporates the historically prominent oyster reefs and shoals that formerly protected inland neighborhoods in the Red Hook/Gowanus Canal region and reintroduces the oyster as a protecting, cleansing, and generative agent in the harbor.

Buttermilk Channel

Red Hook

New Gowanus

Palisade Reef State Park

Erie Basin

Sunset Park

Archipelago

Intertidal reef

Subtidal reef

Navigation channel

Bay Ridge Flats

Wave attenuation

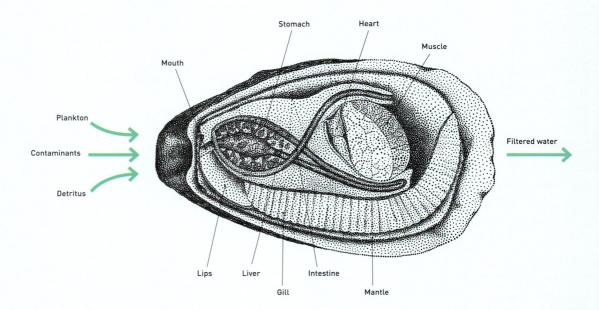

Stomach

Heart

Muscle

Mouth

Plankton

Contaminants

Detritus

Filtered water

Lips

Liver

Intestine

Gill

Mantle

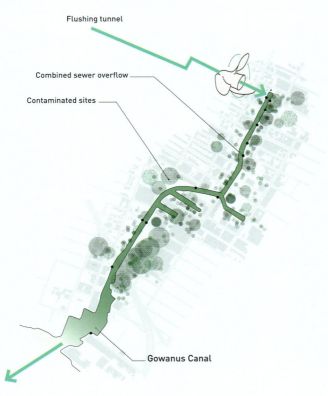

Flushing tunnel

Combined sewer overflow

Contaminated sites

Gowanus Canal

GOWANUS AS FLUPSY

At the north end of the Gowanus Canal, a large propeller pulls in water from Buttermilk Channel via a flushing tunnel. Like a floating upwelling system (FLUPSY) oyster nursery—which increases the growth and viability of young oysters by drawing nutrient-rich water up through the mesh bottom of submerged chambers to feed them continuously—the canal provides an enriched habitat for the growth of shellfish larvae and spats. The young oysters are transferred to a fuzzy-rope-and-timber reef in the Bay Ridge Flats. As they multiply, they strengthen and enlarge the reef, which attenuates storm surges in the subtidal and intertidal zones. An archipelago above the high-water line further calms the water and forms an intricate network of ecological sanctuaries.

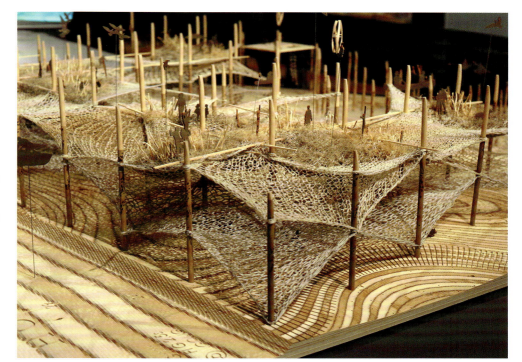

OPPOSITE: Overview and details of model showing the fuzzy-rope-and-timber structure of the oyster reef from above, aquaculture beneath the reef, and the recreational and community opportunities that emerge as a result of reef culture.

TOP: Model detailing reef structure.

RIGHT BOTTOM: Oyster harvesting and recreation in the Bay Ridge Flats.

BELOW: Reef model with background schematic in the gallery.

Q&A

WHAT ASPECTS OF *ON THE WATER* HELPED YOU FRAME YOUR PROJECT? DID YOU EVER DEPART FROM THE ANALYSIS OUTLINED IN *ON THE WATER*?

Kate Orff, SCAPE

Rather than thinking solely about responses to global warming from an engineering or design standpoint, our approach to these concepts took advantage of community-based models for change. Embedded in SCAPE's philosophy is the integration of behavioral change with physical interventions in the urban landscape. We're looking to synthesize design, communication, and participation strategies that are not top-down technomanagerial solutions but dispersed and integrated actions with cumulative effects that generate knowledge and further action. Devising dynamic, flexible landscape infrastructures that make our cities resilient in the face of climate turmoil and generate grassroots commitment (potentially keeping us from reaching those worst-case scenarios!) is the real challenge to us as designers.

A key concept in *On the Water* was the embrace of "soft infrastructure." Since Olmsted's transformation of the Boston Fens in 1887, landscape architects have been looking at green infrastructure relative to public space, sanitation, and water quality. Beyond "soft," SCAPE began to explore biological and dispersed micro-infrastructural models.

Another concept in *On the Water* was the reframing of the Inner Bay as the region's center. I spent two years working on *Envisioning Gateway* (2006), a study that looked at Jamaica Bay and the Gateway National Recreation Area. This led to a competition focusing on the Outer Bay and its marshes and barrier islands. So, seeing the crop of the Outer Bay was initially distressing, especially since a huge percentage of the regional population affected by climate change was therefore placed outside of the *On the Water* study area. Regardless of the frame, the study's overall shift of focus from land to our shared watery fabric will jumpstart the transformation process.

Q2

HOW DOES THIS PROJECT DIFFER FROM YOUR PRACTICE TO DATE?

We believe that engaging climate change is necessarily interdisciplinary and, more importantly, should be intergenerational. We reached out to the New York Harbor School, a local high school, with the thought that its biology teachers and certified student divers would have greater insight into harbor dynamics than your typical engineer or expert. They had amazing ideas and enthusiasm and raised the bar in terms of who we were designing for. We also engaged an older generation of seasoned scientists and advocates, like Bart Chezar and Paul Mankiewicz, who offered insight, context, and hands-on experience.

The workshop experience at MoMA PS1 was consistent with the academic design approach of SCAPE and the experimental but officelike tone of my Columbia University teaching. My team formed a sort of brain trust, each member having a different realm of representational and research expertise. I respected their collective and individual work. This kept our project intensely focused and jovial at the same time.

Q3

WHAT ASPECTS OF YOUR PROJECT WOULD YOU DEVELOP OR CHANGE?

Several ideas were literally left on the workshop table so that the approach to the exhibition would be legible. We developed a comprehensive planning manual for the entire Gowanus/Red Hook upland watershed community that wasn't included. Finalizing and distributing this user-friendly manual would be at the top of my list for further development.

I'd also like to model the hydrodynamics of our proposed reef and develop its form relative to protecting the inner harbor from storm events. I'd overlay this with a more detailed blue-green public-space mosaic. Incorporating data to describe the reef as essential to New York's new infrastructure would help fund the project and move it forward.

Q4

WHAT ASPECTS OF YOUR PROJECT ARE SPECIFIC TO NEW YORK, AND WHAT WOULD BE VALUABLE FOR OTHER CITIES FACING SEA LEVEL RISE?

Harnessing the biological power of keystone species (in New York's case, oysters, eelgrass, and mussels) and organizing the cumulative power of everyday actions are strategies that apply to coastal cities and marine systems worldwide. The idea of "reef culture"—the new public realm formed around an intricate watery network of ecological sanctuary and recreation spaces—is also something that coastal cities can look to as a model. There is a latent, forgotten connection to the water that could be rebuilt as part of urban culture.

Q5

HOW WOULD YOU FORMULATE THE BRIEF IF YOU WERE DESIGNING A COMPETITION LIKE THIS ONE FOR ALL OF NEW YORK CITY, NOT JUST YOUR OWN ZONE?

What became evident in *Rising Currents* is not that we are deficient in ideas, but rather that we lack the political will and the regulatory and legal frameworks to change our relationship to the water. Connecting networks of people to networks of ecology and to the state is crucial. Rather than a design competition, I'd propose a regulatory summit for the Brave Blue World that involves city agencies, New Jersey's and New York's Departments of Environmental Protection, the US Army Corps of Engineers, and the US Environmental Protection Agency. It's astonishing that we can drill for oil 200 miles from shore in thousands of feet of pristine water but we can't experiment with basic research platforms or oyster beds in a deeply compromised urban harbor. Climate science is still in formation, and pilot projects can make design a key part of both scientific development and cultural adaptation.

Q6

WHAT DO YOU THINK THE FUTURE HOLDS FOR ARCHITECTS WORKING ON SEA LEVEL RISE AND CLIMATE CHANGE AND FOR PUBLIC OFFICIALS, BUILDING DEVELOPERS, AND CITIZENS?

The main question I got about Oyster-tecture from politicians and community members was "Why aren't we doing this now?" We're in the beginning stages of working as part of a large team with a group of activists, scientists, and agency staff to develop the reef on the Bay Ridge Flats. Our core concept, of "growing" climate-change infrastructure biologically now rather than relying on capital-intensive big construction projects in the distant future, is our most important message. We can start building ecologies, recreational spaces, and storm-mitigation landscapes that improve water quality and address storm surges. The future will always be uncertain, but these ideas can have an immediate impact.

OPPOSITE: Renderings, models, and photographs of Oyster-tecture in the gallery.

NEW AQUEOUS CITY

ERIC BUNGE AND MIMI HOANG, nARCHITECTS

The team led by Eric Bunge and Mimi Hoang of nARCHITECTS worked on the largest and most varied of the five zones, composed of the heights on both sides of the Verrazano-Narrows Bridge (in Bay Ridge, Brooklyn, and Fort Worth, Staten Island) and a low-lying area of Sunset Park, Brooklyn, to the north.

New Aqueous City creates a novel urban paradigm: a city that can control and absorb rising sea level even as it accommodates an expected spike in population growth over the next century. In counterpoint to an earlier generation's infrastructure, embodied by the Verrazano-Narrows Bridge, this project blurs the boundaries between land and sea, extending the city into the water. Habitable wave-attenuating piers (supporting housing, public leisure areas, and protected wetlands) provide docking points for a network of biogas ferries, and an archipelago of man-made islands connected by inflatable storm barriers encourages silt accumulation, fostering natural resilience against storm surges. At the same time, the water is extended into the city, which is punctuated by a network of infiltration basins, swales, and culverts that absorb storm runoff and function as parks in dry weather. Underlying a host of planning and design suggestions is the assumption of government investment in transformative infrastructure. The ferries and a new tramway supplement existing rapid transit, part of a dynamic infrastructure that works with nature rather than against it.

TEAM MEMBERS
Julia Chapman and Seung Teak Lee, nARCHITECTS; Meir Lobaton Corona, Bureau MLC; Noah Z. Levy, NZL studio; and Sanjukta Sen

PROJECT SITE
Sunset Park, Bay Ridge, and Staten Island

OPPOSITE: New Aqueous City water-flow map showing islands, inflatable barriers, and transportation systems (tramway and ferry lines) in relief. The range of blues in the bay, from dark to light, indicates the depth of the water, from deepest to shallowest.

Storm barriers between man-made islands are inflated when storm-surge flooding occurs.

SUNSET PARK

BAY RIDGE

101

OPPOSITE: New coastal housing is suspended from a roof system that incorporates shared public space. The structural supports double as anaerobic digesters for solid waste and the gas created by the process fuels cooking utilities for each housing block. Floating wetlands transform wet waste into clean water.

TOP: Panels in the exhibition outline aspects of the proposal.

BOTTOM: Detail of model showing hanging houses and treatment wetlands.

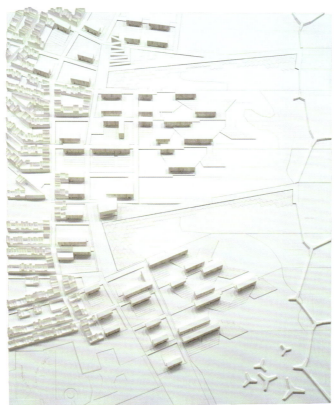

ZONING RESOLUTION

A series of comprehensive regulations for the design of structures and public spaces are presented as a zoning resolution, part of a strategy to incorporate environmental policy into the overall proposal. Details of the resolution (below and pp. 106–107) focus on the wave-attenuating islands and inflatable barriers, public waterfront areas, and new neighborhoods.

DESIGN REQUIREMENTS FOR ISLANDS

Within the zone where the mean sea level is 30 to 40 feet (9.1–12.2 m) above the seabed, no structures other than wave-attenuating islands shall be built.

CONSTRUCTION REQUIREMENTS FOR ISLANDS

Wave-attenuating islands shall be assembled from modular floating sections inflated for transport then brought together by barges. Sections will be equipped with inlet valves to assist in submersion to the riverbed.

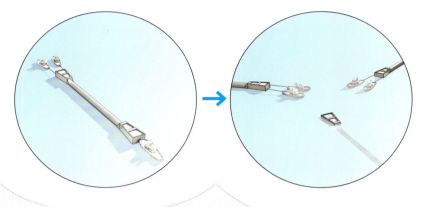

DESIGN REQUIREMENTS FOR INFLATABLE BARRIERS

Wave-attenuating islands shall house a system of inflatable storm barriers. Modular concrete sills on the riverbed will connect individual islands to form an archipelago. In the event of a storm, sensors will signal pumps housed in the concrete islands to inflate the dynamic barriers above the surge water level. Upstream valves will be opened to allow water to enter the tubes. Only during a storm will the archipelago become a defensive line.

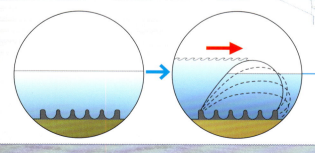

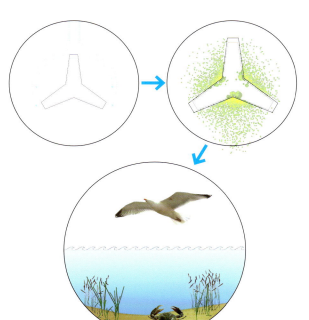

PROVISIONS FOR HABITAT

Wave-attenuating islands, in conjunction with a porous zone of boulders around them, shall be designed to capture sediment flowing down the Hudson River during low tide. Any resulting natural habitat will be protected and allowed to enhance the islands' wave-attenuating properties.

DESIGN REQUIREMENTS FOR PUBLIC WATERFRONT AREAS

Pathways between existing subway stations and ferry docking points shall be zoned as urban development corridors. They will terminate in public waterfront areas resilient to sea level rise and storm surges, encouraging lively, multiple-use neighborhoods and promoting job creation.

DESIGN AND CONSTRUCTION REQUIREMENTS FOR WAVE-ATTENUATING PIERS

Wave-attenuating piers shall extend from urban development corridors. They will support ferry stations, docking facilities, public leisure areas, and protected wetlands. Piers will be composed of boardwalk segments supported on modular porous-concrete wave deflectors (storm-surge side), and floating segments tethered to piles (protected side).

REQUIREMENTS FOR FERRY SERVICE

Biogas ferries shall dock at the wave-attenuating piers—express lines on the water side and local lines on the land side.

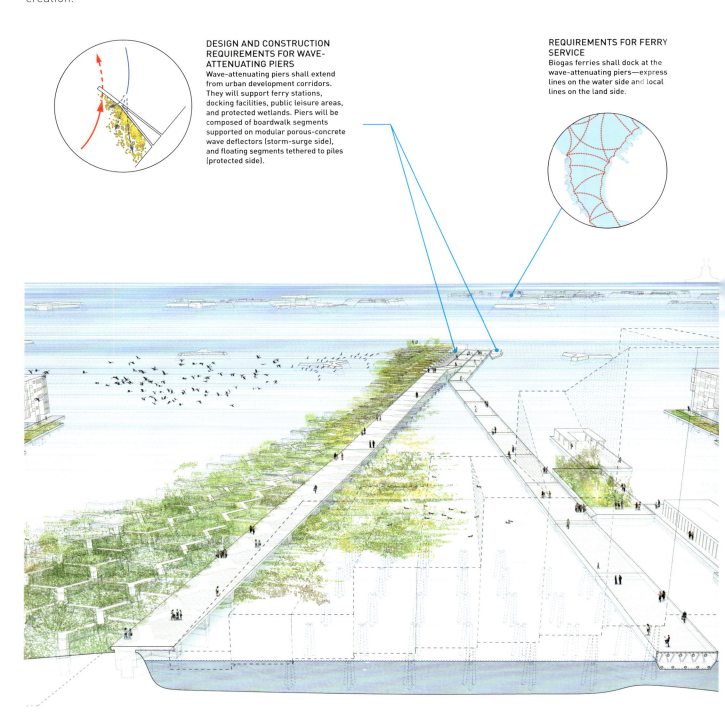

DESIGN REQUIREMENTS FOR AQUEOUS NEIGHBORHOODS

Land less than 20 feet (6.1 m) above mean sea level is subject to flooding during a Category 3 storm. Buildings sited in these areas shall be hung from a shared bridge structure provided by the city. The structure will serve as a safe evacuation zone during flooding, accessed from the uppermost level below the roof via vertical support units that house elevator and stair cores and other amenities. Buildings will be constructed of lightweight materials.

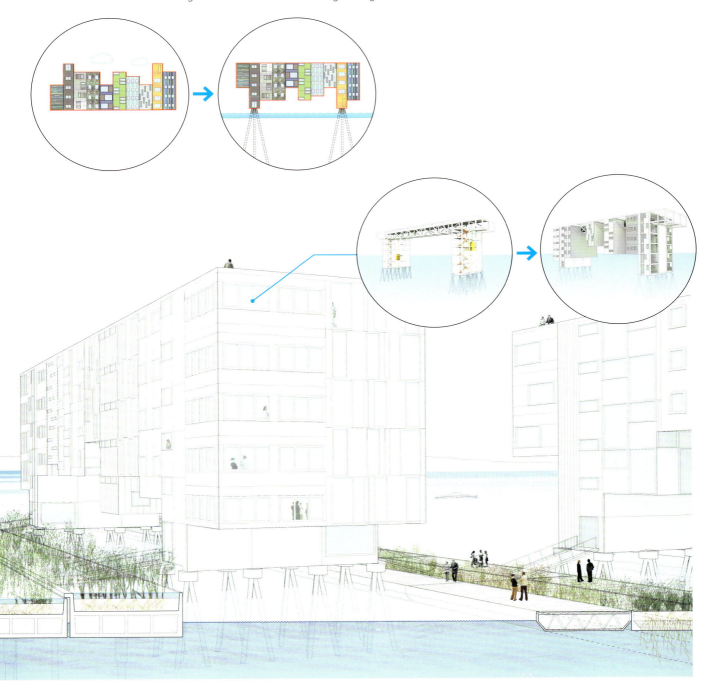

Q&A

WHAT ASPECTS OF *ON THE WATER* HELPED YOU FRAME YOUR PROJECT? DID YOU EVER DEPART FROM THE ANALYSIS OUTLINED IN *ON THE WATER*?

Eric Bunge and Mimi Hoang, nARCHITECTS

On the Water introduced two concepts that provoked reflection about the relationship between cities and ecology: the notion of "soft infrastructure" as a more resilient alternative to "hard" engineering solutions, and the idea of shifting the center of the city from land to water. This latter concept not only challenges notions about the limits and organization of cities but also proposes engaging with at-risk areas to produce resiliency to storm surges and sea level rise while accommodating density in a city projected to grow by one million inhabitants in the next two decades. Rather than introduce a purely ecological/leisure buffer zone, therefore, we attempted to bring the city to the water and have the city accommodate the water in ecological ways.

We departed from *On the Water* in seeing a continuing role for hard engineering solutions in conjunction with strategies of soft infrastructure. One example of our attempt to reconcile these approaches was our proposal to connect artificial islands with dynamically inflatable barriers—this approach remains soft within the study's definition of a resilient and reversible solution that minimizes the impact on ecology, but it does incorporate elements of engineering that might be categorized as hard.

Q2

HOW DOES THIS PROJECT DIFFER FROM YOUR PRACTICE TO DATE?

In our office we pursue a nonlinear, multipronged approach that accommodates failure and allows for quick leaps forward or backward. Feedback from outside entities occurs in a structured way, allowing us some measure of control on how the feedback is incorporated in our work.

In contrast, the open workshop introduced a linear, fast-paced framework, within which a large number of people could participate in real time; we often likened the experience to the TV series *Project Runway*. Our entire process became both product and message. This required a different editorial approach in our search for rigor and conceptual clarity. In the end, the issues that inform a project are not necessarily those that the project addresses.

Q3

WHAT ASPECTS OF YOUR PROJECT WOULD YOU DEVELOP OR CHANGE?

We are interested in pursuing further the notion of acupunctural urbanism—a term borrowed from a former mayor of Curitiba, Brazil, Jaime Lerner. We took the position that a large number of actors need to be corralled when considering a wide-reaching transformation of cities, from government agencies to market forces to local communities. We envisaged a city that would become resilient to sea level rise and storm surges through the gradual implementation of a series of nodes dispersed across a large area. In counterpoint to the totalizing solutions of previous generations, these nodes, or seeds, as we began to call them, would in theory sponsor several kinds of transformations, accommodating not only ecological growth, but also changing technologies and evolving mind-sets.

We focused on three kinds of seeds: archipelagoes interconnected with dynamically inflatable barriers, piers extending land-based transportation out into the water, and bridgelike structures that would allow the suspension of lightweight housing over the water—to depths determined by residents' appetite for risk. Each of these sponsored two kinds of growth by accretion: the natural growth of cities around infrastructural armatures and the actual growth of habitat. We hope to eventually build some experimental seeds and document their transformation.

Q4

WHAT ASPECTS OF YOUR PROJECT ARE SPECIFIC TO NEW YORK, AND WHAT WOULD BE VALUABLE FOR OTHER CITIES FACING SEA LEVEL RISE?

"Run for the hills!" This was the advice given to us by an engineer visiting our workshop at MoMA PS1. He is one of the authors of a series of proposed storm-surge dams that would effectively close off the harbor—a solution that would most likely alter the ecology of the bay with disastrous consequences but that in his opinion could stave off the kind of catastrophe that happened in New Orleans as a result of Hurricane Katrina. In many population centers geographically similar to New York, running for the hills is not feasible. Moreover, it continues an attitude of sequestration from the environment that hard engineering solutions have tried to control—the urban equivalent of central air-conditioning. From the point of view of the exhibition's mandate, running for the hills would also miss opportunities for ingenuity.

In these general ways, *Rising Currents* could be understood as prototypical. However, it is precisely a disengagement from local conditions that has produced a detached set of engineering principles that have not proved resilient in all cases. Each city should study the issue from its own unique set of environmental, cultural, and technical frameworks.

Q5

HOW WOULD YOU FORMULATE THE BRIEF IF YOU WERE DESIGNING A COMPETITION LIKE THIS ONE FOR ALL OF NEW YORK CITY, NOT JUST YOUR OWN ZONE?

Not very differently. We saw our zone as a window onto a possible future city, which we named New Aqueous City in a pun that references the heroic projects of the 1960s, to which we viewed our project as antithetical. Many of the systems we developed and represented—whether the biogas ferries powered by sewage or the mobile programmed barges docking at piers—make sense at the scale of a regional city. We would formulate the competition brief to get at the way cities actually evolve, which we don't see as a design exercise predicated on a delineated site.

Q6

WHAT DO YOU THINK THE FUTURE HOLDS FOR ARCHITECTS WORKING ON SEA LEVEL RISE AND CLIMATE CHANGE AND FOR PUBLIC OFFICIALS, BUILDING DEVELOPERS, AND CITIZENS?

Architects should address their multiple roles as facilitators of climate change, communicators about human impact, and inventors proposing solutions. Not everyone can or needs to work on everything all at once! But architects have an ability and responsibility to reach out to other disciplines and invent new frameworks for addressing the problem.

OPPOSITE: New Aqueous City models, renderings, and stills from illustrative animations in the gallery.

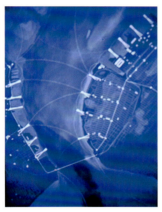

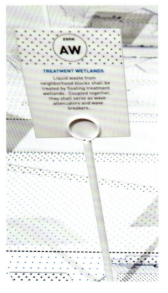

ACKNOWLEDGMENTS

The *Rising Currents* workshop and exhibition were collaborations between a great many people and organizations. We apologize for any oversights in our long roster of thanks; the teams worked with many valuable contributors who, due to space constraints, are not named individually here.

For their crucial support we wish first to thank Glenn D. Lowry, Director, and the board of trustees of The Museum of Modern Art. We also extend our gratitude to the exhibition's sponsors, the Rockefeller Foundation and Andre Singer.

Guy Nordenson and Catherine Seavitt lent their considerable enthusiasm and expertise to the project from its inception to its conclusion, and for this we are truly appreciative. We also thank Rebecca Veit and Elizabeth Hodges of Guy Nordenson and Associates for their assistance.

We are particularly grateful to the leaders of the departments at the Museum and MoMA PS1 who helped make *Rising Currents* happen: Ramona Bannayan, Deputy Director for Exhibitions and Collections; Maria DeMarco Beardsley, Coordinator of Exhibitions; Klaus Biesenbach, Director of MoMA PS1; Todd Bishop, Director, Exhibition Funding and MoMA PS1 Development; Julia Hoffmann, Creative Director, Advertising and Graphic Design; Rob Jung, Manager, and Sarah Wood, Assistant Manager, Department of Art Handling and Preparation; Jerry Neuner, Director, Department of Exhibition Design and Production; and Wendy Woon, Deputy Director for Education.

We are grateful to the members of the jury who generously volunteered their time and expertise: David Adjaye, founder, Adjaye Associates, London; Klaus Biesenbach; Amanda Burden, Chair, New York City Planning Commission; Antonio Guerrero, former Director of Operations and Exhibitions, MoMA PS1; Glenn D. Lowry; Professor Guy Nordenson of Princeton University; Professor Michael Oppenheimer of Princeton University; and Peter Reed, Senior Deputy Director for Curatorial Affairs, MoMA.

The team leaders, members, and consultants all worked tirelessly to bring their projects to completion despite challenging time constraints and logistical complexities. We extend our thanks to Stephen Cassell and Adam Yarinsky of Architecture Research Office and Susannah C. Drake of dlandstudio, with team members Lauren Barry, Yong K. Kim, Neil Patel, Elliott Landry Smith, Leah Kiren Solk, and Michael Jejon Yeung and additional contributors David Anderson, Taryn Harunah, Kara Lanahan, Erica Layton, Ken Missbrenner, Charles C. W. Smith, and Michael Yarinsky; Paul Lewis, Marc Tsurumaki, and David J. Lewis of LTL Architects, with team members Aaron Forrest, Megan Griscom, Perla Dís Kristinsdóttir, and Yasmin Vobis and additional contributors Phillip Chang, Laura Cheung, Hye-Young Chung, Jason Dannenbring, Cody Fithian, Yu-Cheng Koh, Amanda Kronk, Paul Landon, Mia Lorenzetti Lee, Clark Manning, Deric Mizokami, John Morrison, and Luke Smith; Matthew Baird of Matthew Baird Architects, with team members Kira Appelhans, Kristen Becker, Daniel Greenfield, Nim Lee, Ajay Manthripragada, Maria Milans del Bosch, and Juanita Wichienkuer and consultants Hank Adams, Atelier Ten, Teresa Ball, Amanda Bayley, Juliette Bensimon-Marchina, Alan Blumberg, Kate Boicourt,

Mark Dion, eDesign Dynamics, Tom Flagg, Alex Guerrero, Stephen Iino, Joy Kang, Bradley Kaye, Mike Koller, Wendy Meguro, Erik Muller, Gerhardt Muller, Ellen Neises, Mike Novogratz, Sukey Novogratz, Nat Oppenheimer, Margot Otten, Jorge Pereira, Richard Plunz, Andreas Rasmussen, Matthew Ritchie, Eric Rothstein, Philip Simmons, Cassie Spieler, Maria-Paola Sutto, Billie Tsien, Shanta Tucker, Wheaton Arts and Cultural Center, Tod Williams, Bryan Wilson, Dimitri Yacubov, and Ted Zoli; Eric Bunge and Mimi Hoang of nARCHITECTS, with team members Julia Chapman, Meir Lobaton Corona, Seung Teak Lee, Noah Z. Levy, and Sanjukta Sen and additional contributors Brett Appel, ARUP NY, Margaret Garcia, Rebecca Garnett, Dominique Gonfard, Andre Guimond, Steven Hagmann, Buro Happold, Matthew Herman, Anuradha Mathur and Dilip da Cunha, Mathur/da Cunha, Hubert Pelletier, Ed Purver, Teo Quintana, Juliana Muniz, Mahadev Raman, Varanesh Singh, Cameron Thomson, Tyler Velten; and Kate Orff of SCAPE, with team members Ben Abelman, Angela Chen-Mai Soong, Alice Feng, Steven Garcia, and Geneva Wirth and additional contributors Deborah Barr, Elena Brescia, Bart Chezar, Glen Cummings, Habu Textiles, Laurie Hawkinson, Linda La Belle, David Lefkowitz, Pete Malinowski, Paul Mankiewicz, Katie Mosher-Smith, Sri Rangarajan, Phil Simmons, SITU Studio, the New York Harbor School, and Uhuru Design.

Both MoMA and MoMA PS1 provided crucial support and guidance for the organization of the unprecedented workshop-and-exhibition format of the project. At MoMA, we thank Nancy Adelson, Deputy General Counsel; Glenn D. Lowry; and Jennifer Russell, former Senior Deputy Director of Exhibitions. At MoMA PS1, we thank Sixto Figueroa, Director of Building Services; Antonio Guerrero; Yun Joo Kang, Chief Administrative Officer; Christopher Y. Lew, Assistant Curator; Sarah Scandiffio, Special Events Manager and Curatorial Assistant for Public Programs; and Anna Dabney Smith, Visitor Services Manager. All made special initiatives for the project, for which we are grateful. Special thanks are extended also to Hunter Palmer, Project Manager, who, assisted by intern Jenny Shen, facilitated the workshops at MoMA PS1 with dedication.

In MoMA's Department of Publications we extend our gratitude to Christopher Hudson, Publisher; Kara Kirk, Associate Publisher; Marc Sapir, Production Director; and David Frankel, Editorial Director; as well as Rebecca Roberts, Senior Assistant Editor, and Libby Hruska, Editor, for their diligent editing; Tiffany Hu, Production Manager; and Hannah Kim, Marketing Coordinator. Our thanks to Julia Hoffman and Hsien-yin Ingrid Chou, Assistant Creative Director, Department of Advertising and Graphic Design, the catalogue's designer, who did a wonderful job of weaving elements from the exhibition design into the book.

From our exhibition team we thank, in particular, Jerry Neuner, who oversaw the design of this exhibition; Lana Hum, Production Manager, Department of Exhibition Design and Production; Hsien-yin Ingrid Chou; and Steven Wheeler, Assistant Registrar.

We are grateful to MoMA's Department of Information Technology, especially K Mita, Director, Audio/Visual Services, and Howard Deitch, Mike Gibbons, Lucas Gonzales, Charlie Kalinowski, Nathaniel Longcope, and Bjorn Quenemoen. In the Department of Digital Media, we thank Allegra Burnette, Creative Director, and Shannon

CREDITS

Darrough, David Hart, and Dan Phiffer. In the Department of Marketing, our appreciation goes to Rebecca Stokes, Director, Digital Marketing Communications, and Jason Persse, Associate Editor, Development and Membership.

In the Department of Architecture and Design we are grateful for the support we enjoyed from the entire staff. We give special thanks to Colin Hartness, Assistant to the Chief Curator; Dara Kiese, former Curatorial Assistant; Whitney May, Department Assistant; and Margot Weller, Curatorial Assistant.

Also at the Museum, we extend grateful appreciation to Michael Margitich, Senior Deputy Director for External Affairs; Todd Bishop, Director of Exhibition Funding; Elizabeth Burke, Foundation Relations Director; Melissa Kirschner, Assistant to the Senior Deputy Director for External Affairs; Heidi Speckhart, Development Officer; and Lauren Stakias, Assistant Director, Exhibition Funding. Thanks also to Kim Mitchell, Director of Communications, Advertising, and Graphics; Margaret Doyle, Director, Communications; Meg Blackburn, former Senior Publicist; and Kim Donica, Publicity Coordinator. In the Department of Education, special thanks go to Wendy Woon; Sara Bodinson, Director, Interpretation and Research; and Pablo Helguera, Director, and Laura Beiles, Assistant Director, Adult and Academic Programs.

We also wish to recognize the contributions of the following people inside and outside the Museum, with thanks: Michele Arms, Karlyn Benson, Claire Corey, Elizabeth Graham, Matthea Harvey, Robert Kastler, Tom Krueger, Erik Landsberg, Maria Marchenkova, Chris McGlinchey, Bryan Reyna, Roberto Rivera, and Olivia Striffler. We extend a special thanks to our colleagues at partner organizations who helped support the project with their generous gifts of time and expertise: Nicholas Anderson, Rick Bell, Adrian Benepe, Amanda Burden, Joan K. Davidson, Adam Freed, Rosalie Genevro, Adriaan Geuze, Leslie Koch, Cecilia Kushner, Marie O'Shea, Ben Prosky, Anne Rieselbach, Sarah Romanowski, Cristina Rumbaitis del Rio, Abby Suckle, Daniel Teitelbaum, Edwin Torres, Bill Woods, and Tom Wright.

Lastly, my gratitude and thanks to Emma Presler, Department Manager, Department of Architecture and Design, for her dedication and commitment to this project that expanded in scope and influence in ways that far exceeded our expectations.

Barry Bergdoll
THE PHILIP JOHNSON CHIEF CURATOR,
DEPARTMENT OF ARCHITECTURE AND DESIGN

NOTES

1. United Nations Population Fund, *State of World Population 2007: Unleashing the Potential of Urban Growth,* 2007, http://www.unfpa.org/public/home/publications/pid/408.
2. Guoming Wen, "Cautions on China's Urbanization," Maureen and Mike Mansfield Foundation, January 11, 2005, http://www.mansfieldfdn.org/pubs/pub_pdfs/wen0105_chinaurban.pdf.
3. "IPCC, 2007: Summary for Policymakers," in S. Solomon, D. Qin, M. Manning, Z. Chen, M. Marquis, K. B. Averyt, M. Tignor, and H. L. Miller, eds., *Climate Change 2007: Working Group I: The Physical Science Basis. Contribution of Working Group I to the Fourth Assessment Report of the Intergovernmental Panel on Climate Change* (Cambridge and New York: Cambridge University Press, 2007), http://www.ipcc.ch/publications_and_data/ar4/wg1/en/spm.html.
4. M. P. Cooper, M. D. Beevers, and M. Oppenheimer, "The Potential Impacts of Sea Level Rise on the Coastal Region of New Jersey, USA," *Climatic Change* 90 (2008): 475–92, doi:10.1007/s10584-008-9422-0.
5. Jason P. Ericson et al., "Effective Sea-Level Rise and Deltas: Causes of Change and Human Dimension Implications," *Global and Planetary Change* 50, no. 1–2 (2006): 63–82, doi:10.1016/j.gloplacha.2005.07.004.
6. Mark P. McCarthy et al., "Climate Change in Cities Due to Global Warming and Urban Effects," *Geophysical Research Letters* 37 (May 8, 2010), L09705, doi:10.1029/2010GL042845.
7. Peter Stott et al., "Human Contribution to the European Heatwave of 2003," *Nature* 432 (December 2, 2004): 610–14, doi:10.1038/nature03089.
8. S. Feng, A. Krueger, M. Oppenheimer, "Linkages Among Climate Change, Crop Yields and Mexico–JS Cross-border Migration," *Proceedings of the National Academy of Science* (July 26, 2010), www.pnas.org/cgi/doi/10.1073/pnas.1002632107.
9. *Inventory of United States Greenhouse Gas Emissions and Sinks, 1990–2008,* United States Environmental Protection Agency, 2010, http://www.epa.gov/climatechange/emissions/downloads10/508_Complete_GHG_1990_2008.pdf.
10. Larry Flowers, *Wind Energy Update,* National Renewable Energy Laboratory, 2010, http://www.windpoweringamerica.gov/pdfs/wpa/wpa_update.pdf.
11. E. Rosenthal, "Nations That Debate Coal Use Export It to Feed China's Need," *New York Times,* November 21, 2010, http://www.nytimes.com/2010/11/22/science/earth/22fossil.html.
12. For a summary of China's views on energy, economic growth, and climate change, see *China's National Climate Change Program*, National Development and Reform Commission, People's Republic of China, June 2007, http://www.ccchina.gov.cn/WebSite/CCChina/UpFile/File188.pdf.